The Gastronomical! Guide To...

Fabulous Food!

By Claire Bosi & Petrie Hosken

Illustrations by David Webb

First published in Great Britain in 2014 by
A Way With Media
Shrewsbury SY3 7LN
www.awaywithmedia.com

© Gastronomical! Ltd

ISBN: 978-0-9576292-8-8

Edited, photographed and published by Andrew Richardson
www.awaywithmedia.com

Illustrated by David Webb
Design and editorial production by Rob March
www.wearebeard.com

For Paige and Barnaby

Life loves to be taken by the lapel and told:
"I'm with you, kid. Lets go."

Maya Angelou

Contents

THE FOREWORD
BY TOM KERRIDGE

So many of us these days buy all of our food pre-packed, cellophane wrapped, portion controlled and creatively designed as a marketing tool. But the reality of great food comes from raw ingredients. I remember as a child, visiting butchers, calling in to greengrocers and seeing the fresh fish on market stalls. It's a shame that these small scale, almost artisan suppliers hardly exist anymore, as that is where I gained my massive love and admiration of food - from the raw ingredient.

Standing in an old school greengrocers in different times of the year and seeing how vegetables change, not just in colour, from the bright greens and reds of summer, to the browns, oranges and yellows of autumn - but the smells and flavours.

I can always tell when a young chef is going to become a great chef when they are more excited about seeing the raw ingredient, rather than how it looks on the plate as a finished item. Too often chefs are influenced by fashionable presentation, expensive plates and quirky gimmicks to sell food. For me it should always come down to the raw ingredient, this is by far the most exciting point in the journey of the produce. It allows your imagination to flourish with how you are going to cook the ingredient, the flavours it can create, taking into account all the exciting processes it can go through, or even just serving it raw.

It is never too early to learn about produce. The path that all food produce goes on, from growing, nurturing, picking or slaughtering, is a varied one, where along the way you meet passionate, exciting and hard working people, all with a love of food. This cookery book will help children and young people alike, not only to cook and have an interest in food but, for some, hopefully ignite a lifelong passion for food.

Love Tom Kerridge x

Claire

Petrie

About the authors

Petrie Hosken and Claire Bosi are sisters. Petrie is the older, bossier one which leaves Claire as the younger, much more easy going one! They have three brothers and grew up in the Oxfordshire countryside. Their mother was certainly no cook so don't be thinking these books were inspired by their own childhoods – they were not! Their mother raised them alone and worked full time as a veterinary surgeon. With five hungry mouths to feed it was often easier to turn to pre-prepared food. That's no criticism; it's just the way life was in a busy home.

As the girls grew up, one learned to cook, the other did not. The interesting fact here is that Claire, who decided not to cook, went on to become the founder of one of the best restaurants in the world - the two Michelin-starred Hibiscus. Claire now cooks everyday, but her adventures into the cooking arena only started when she reached her twenties!

Petrie, the older one, loves cooking. Her passion began when she was a very young child. She went on to become a broadcaster, both on radio and television. Talking all the time requires some skill but not as much as turning out the perfect choux bun or chicken curry! Petrie still cooks and is never happier than when she is creating a new dish.

Despite those differences, the sisters they have absolutely identical and silly senses of humour. They make each other laugh a lot – though they are not so sure that the rest of the world is convinced by their 'jokes'! They are such good friends that they finish each other's sentences – but wouldn't dream of finishing each other's wine!

Claire and Petrie are both full time, working mothers.

INTRODUCTION

We cannot live without food. Fact.

As we grow up, we are educated. Our schools, clubs, families and friends all play major parts in creating and crafting the people we become. The experiences we have as children and the things we learn and grasp at an early age go forth with us into adulthood.

So, let's just clear up a few things about cooking:

LEARNING TO COOK CAN BE FUN

Why cooking is not wholeheartedly embraced by all schools is a mystery. It is a life skill. It is one we will use for the rest of our lives – whether we become, actors, doctors or stay-at-home parents, it is essential. We all learn about the mathematical Pi in secondary education but few of us are taught how to actually make a pie. But as adults, being able to make a pie is likely to be of more use to us than being able to measure a circle.

COOKING IS NOT JUST ABOUT BEING IN A KITCHEN

Learning to shop wisely is just as important. We improve our shopping habits as our interest in cooking grows. Having a budget and making sure our diet includes all the essential food groups uses brain power, mathematics, common sense and sometimes (market traders beware!) a little bit of bartering.

ADULTS CAN BE PATRONISING ABOUT FOOD

All adults want children to eat healthily. But the tendency for many of them is to try and make food entertaining in a way that it just isn't. What is a chicken dinosaur, anyway? Why make food into silly shapes, just to encourage children to eat them?

Cooking Responsibly

A kitchen is an area where knives and heat are frequently used and where there is a great deal of family activity. Whilst we encourage young people to get into the kitchen and learn, we advise parents or carers to judge their own child's ability and to supervise, even if from a distance – or from behind a tea towel. There is a great deal of satisfaction and enjoyment in cooking together - once you can see past all the mess, that is.

The recipes

The recipes in the book are ranked in levels, 1 being the simplest and 3 being most complex. They are designed to allow your child to gain confidence in their cooking abilities before moving on to the harder levels.

We always find it best to read through a recipe in full before starting to cook or prepare the food, as it allows us to plan what equipment is required and preheat the oven if we need to. There's nothing worse than getting stuck in and realising that you haven't got something that the recipe needs, so be sure to check!

You may also notice that some recipes call for the use of alcohol. But don't worry, that won't make you drunk. We only ever use very small quantities and most of the alcohol is cooked out as part of the cooking process.

PART 1

THE GASTRONOMICAL! GUIDE TO...

VIRTUOUS BUT VILLAINOUS VEGETABLES AND ROOTS

WHAT IS A VEGETABLE?

Vegetables are classed depending on which part of the plant is eaten. Some vegetables may fall into more than one category when more than one part of the plant is eaten, for example, both the roots and leaves of beetroot can be eaten.

BULBS

Bulbs usually grow just below the surface of the ground and produce a fleshy, leafy shoot above the ground. Bulbs usually consist of layers or clustered segments. Typical examples are onion, shallot, garlic, spring onion, leek and fennel.

FLOWERS

The edible flowers of certain vegetables such as cauliflower, broccoli and globe artichokes.

FRUITS

Vegetable fruit are fleshy and contain seeds for example aubergine, peppers, courgette, okra, pumpkin and tomato.

FUNGI

More commonly known as mushroom, including button, flat, shitake, oyster, gourmet brown, wood ear and truffles. Be warned – there is nothing fun about them – they don't tell jokes or do anything amusing – ever!

Leaves

The edible leaves of plants such as bok choy, cabbage, lettuce and spinach.

Roots

Usually a long or round shape, these include carrot, turnip, beetroot, swede, radish, parsnip and celeriac.

Seeds

Usually obtained from pods which are sometimes eaten along with the seeds these include broad bean, French bean, pea and sugar snap pea.

Stems

The edible stalks of plants when the stalk is the main part of the vegetable. For example asparagus, celery and kohlrabi.

Tubers

Vegetables which grow underground on the root of a plant, for example potato, Jerusalem artichoke and sweet potato.

Reasons for Seasons
- what's in and what's out

In short, the year is divided into four periods, known as seasons. These are spring, summer, autumn **and** winter.

But how do they happen?

Some parts of the year are hotter than others. That's because the sun is closer to the earth at different times of the year. Our dear old planet Earth is a bit wonky: tilted, in fact.

The Earth's axis (an imaginary straight line down the centre of the Earth) is tilted. That means that the Earth is always 'pointing' to one side as it goes around the sun. Sometimes the sun points directly at the earth, but at other times it does not. The different amounts of sunlight illuminating the Earth during the year creates the seasons.

Why are seasons important?

Air and soil temperatures are important for the germination of seeds. All fruit and vegetable plants have different requirements. The garden pea absolutely will not budge in winter and asparagus would also much rather keep its head underground. Can you blame them? It makes sense that root vegetables are in season during the Autumn and Winter months as they live underground, so benefit from the warmth of the soil. Beans and courgettes, however, grow on stalks and so enjoy basking in the summer sunshine!

Spring

Summer

So, as we know, we have natural seasons and the best fruit and vegetables live and grow within those. So that is when we should eat them. Also have you considered that nature has encouraged certain things to grow at the same time? Often they go together so well. Nutty and sweet pumpkins go so well with harvested walnuts and hazelnuts. Juicy tomatoes go beautifully with basil. You could even think about the tender meat of a spring lamb with the grassy flavours of asparagus and the sweet bite that you get from peas.

Years ago, we wouldn't even have this conversation. We ate what was growing naturally at the time. But airfreight and demand for, say, strawberries in January means that at supermarkets you can buy pretty much anything at any time. Raspberries for a Christmas trifle? That's easy these days but it's not appropriate. Stick to independent vegetable shops if you can, or even better, grow your own. You don't need an allotment, just use a garden or a window box.

What's in for spring?

Asparagus, cauliflower, Jersey royal potatoes, purple sprouting broccoli, spinach, spring greens, spring onions (the clue is in the names there!), radishes and watercress.

And for a hummer of a summer?

Aubergine, broad beans, broccoli, beetroot, courgettes, cucumber, carrots, fennel, peas, green beans, lettuce and salad, new potatoes, runner beans, rocket, radishes and tomatoes.

A symptom of autumn?

Beetroot, carrots, celeriac, field mushrooms, some wild mushrooms, kale, leeks, potatoes, pumpkins, squashes (as in butternut - not orange or blackcurrant), sweetcorn, tomatoes and watercress.

Who's a sprinter for winter?

Brussel sprouts, cabbages, celeriac, cauliflower, chicory, artichokes, leeks, parsnips, potatoes, red cabbage, swede and turnips.

Autumn

Winter

Nature gets the picture, why don't we?

It appears that Mother Nature has, for centuries, been leaving us direct clues as to what is good for us - and in the simplest of ways. Check out the shape of these vegetables and fruits to the area of the body they benefit.

Carrot

A carrot, sliced widthways resembles a human eye with a pupil, an iris and radiating lines. Science now proves that eating carrots enhances blood flow to and function of your eyes.

Kidney Beans

Kidney beans, well they look like kidneys and are extremely efficient in maintaining healthy kidney function.

Avocados & Pears

Avocados and pears target the health and function of the female womb and cervix. Research shows that if a woman eats 1 avocado a week, it balances hormones, helps lose baby weight and helps prevent cervical cancer. How profound then, that it takes exactly 9 months for an avocado to grow from blossom to fully ripe fruit.

Celery & Rhubarb

Celery and Rhubarb look like bones. Bones are 23% sodium and celery is 23% sodium. If you don't have enough sodium in your diet then your body will take it from your bones, making them weak.

Tomato

A tomato has four chambers and is red. A human heart has four chambers and is red. Research again shows that tomatoes are loaded with lycopine and are pure heart and blood food.

Grapes

Grapes hang in a cluster that has the shape of the heart. Each grape looks like a blood cell and all of the research today shows grapes are also profound heart and blood vitalising food.

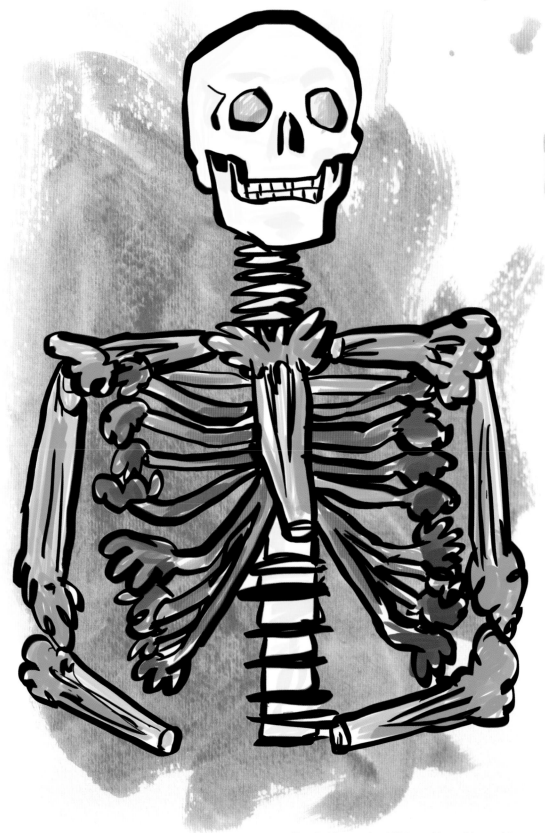

POTATOES

Potatoes are the most important source of vitamin C in our modern diet. That is ironic given that, at one time, they were feared because they are classified in the same botanical family as nightshade (the deadly variety). It was only after potatoes became one of our staple foods in the 18th century that scurvy began to die out! Most of us will eat a potato every day in one form or another. Roasted, mashed, boiled, baked, jacketed and most popular of all, chipped!

WHY? The potato is rich in protein, carbohydrates, minerals, and vitamins such as riboflavin, niacin and Vitamin C. It's therefore possible, but not recommended, to stay healthy on a diet of potatoes alone - though not on a diet of chips so don't try that one!

HOW... Mashed, boiled, chipped, roast, scalloped, crisps. Potatoes are great as a main ingredient, for example baked, or as an inclusion in a dish, for example in a soup. The humble potato is perhaps the most versatile of vegetables.

HISTORY

The potato was introduced to Britain by Sir Francis Drake in 1585/6 when he presented it to Queen Elizabeth I. The explorer and politician had, a year earlier, set sail with his ships for the West Indies. His intention was to steal Spanish treasures and gold for Queen Elizabeth. Having burned, looted and stomped his way through the islands he returned a year later with no treasures, just potatoes and tobacco.

King Frederick II of Prussia was so convinced of the nutritional value of potatoes that he threatened to cut off the ears and noses of his subjects if they refused to grow them.

Louis XVI of France wore potato flowers in his buttonhole to stimulate interest in the plant.

In the 1700s, agronomist Antoine-Auguste Parmentier used reverse psychology to convince the French to accept the potato as a safe food. He posted guards around potato fields during the day to prevent people from stealing them - but left those same fields unguarded at night. Every night, thieves would sneak into the fields and leave with sacks of potatoes.

Killer Potatoes

In a bleak and gruesome chapter in Irish history, diseased potatoes killed over a million men, women and children and caused another million to flee the country. To be fair it was the famine and disease that killed them – the potato just became too rotten to eat!

By the 1800s, more than 3 million Irish peasants lived on a diet of just potatoes and not much else. The famine began quite mysteriously in September 1845 with a disease called 'The Blight'. It spread rapidly throughout the potato fields, turning plants black and as they rotted, they let off a revolting stench.

Without potatoes, the Irish in the countryside began to live off wild blackberries, nettles, turnips, cabbage leaves, edible seaweed, shellfish, roots, roadside weeds and even grass.

The Great British Chip

✓ If you laid all the British potatoes that are turned into chips every year end to end, they would stretch around the world 76 times and would weigh the equivalent of 2.9 million Formula 1 cars.

✓ 1 out of every 4 British potatoes are made into chips – that's approximately 1.5 million tonnes every year. That means that 10% of the entire British potato crop is needed to supply all the fish and chip shops and it would take an area the size of 56,000 football pitches to grow all the potatoes needed for the chips consumed in Great Britain each year.

Root Vegetables

Root vegetables are plant roots used as vegetables and we love 'em. There's even a jelly bean flavour for carrots now.

Root vegetables are storage organs, essentially the larder for the plant that grows above. They are full of starch, sugar and carbohydrates.

In Britain, they tend to be in season in autumn and winter. They are crammed full of vitamins and minerals and their nutty, earthy flavours are great for soups, roasts and other warming dishes popular at that time of year.

Well known examples of easily available root vegetables are parsnips, carrots, beetroot, swedes and radish.

Roots Manuva, is a British rapper from Stockwell, South London. His real name is Rodney Hylton Smith. He's not a root vegetable but has been known to rap about cheese on toast.

CARROTS

Carrots were the first ever vegetable to be commercially canned. Love them or hate them, I bet they are one of the most used root vegetables in your house. The average person will eat approximately over 10,000 carrots over in their lifetime!

The carrot is a member of the parsley family, which includes species such as celery, parsnip, fennel, dill and coriander.

Carrots, which are 87% water, have the highest content of beta carotene (vitamin A) of all vegetables. That's where they get their orange colour from. There is as much calcium in 9 carrots as there is in a glass (250ml) of whole milk. And they help you see in the dark.

Boiled, mashed, puréed, souped, roasted, snowman's nose, stir fried and grated into a cake mix are just some of the uses for carrots.

HISTORY

The early days of the carrot has got carrot historians (yes such people do exist!) all of a tizzy! Some say it is impossible to chart the very early history of the carrot because in the early days, the carrot was white and spindly and a bit woody – a bit like the parsnip.

Originally, carrots came in a variety of colours, from purple and black to yellow and red. Orange carrots did not appear until the 1500's when the Dutch Royal House of Orange was in power. The Dutch therefore decided to breed an orange carrot by using a mutant yellow carrot seed from North Africa combined with a red carrot seed. The newly orange carrots arrived in England via Dutch travellers during the reign of Queen Elizabeth I. They soon caught on in England as both a food and a fashion accessory. Ladies would often use carrot tops to decorate their hats!

Hippocrates created a broth recipe for good health consisting of carrots, celery, root parsley and leeks.

The Ancient Greeks called the carrot a 'philtron', which translates to 'love charm'. They believed the carrot made both men and women more amorous.

Carrot Trivia

- The Anglo-Saxons included carrots as an ingredient in a medicinal drink against the devil and insanity (how mad is that?!)

- China produces 274,900,000 tons of carrots per year.

- The Flaming Carrot was a mysterious and demented comic book superhero.

- A teaspoon will hold almost 2000 carrot seeds.

- The longest carrot recorded in 1996 was 5.14 meters (16 feet 10 ½ inches) and the heaviest carrot recorded in the world 18.985 lb in 1998

- The total area in Britain planted with carrots each year is 9000 hectares - double the size of Holland's carrot production area. That's 2000 times bigger than the roof area of Wembley Stadium or the equivalent of 18,000 football pitches.

- A 2005 poll revealed that carrots are the third most popular vegetable in Britain. Brussel sprouts are the least popular.

PARSNIPS

As we have already discovered, many years ago the carrot and the parsnip looked similar and were often confused as the same vegetable. Today, however, they are very different in look as well as flavour. Parsnips look like a pale carrot and indeed are a relative of the carrot, as well as celeriac, and parsley root. When roasted, parsnips caramelise very well and are sweet in flavour – delicious!

Parsnips are commonly found across Europe and grow best in cool climate regions. Parsnips have a celery-like nutty flavour. They taste best in the winter and develop a sweet taste after two weeks storage. Water hemlock is sometimes confused with parsnip since it looks similar - but is a poisonous root.

Richer than carrots in vitamins and minerals, parsnips are also extremely high in potassium.

Roasted with a drizzle of honey, mmm. Boiled, mashed, puréed, baked and sautéed.

Turnip

We know many children (and some adults) don't really like the taste of turnips but it is one of those flavours that you are likely to grow in to. Before potatoes were abundant, turnips were an everyday staple food. The turnip has a reddish/cream skin and looks like a huge radish. In fact, they are part of the same family.

Packed full of Vitamins B6, C + K, lots of dietary fibre and potassium, turnips helps to keep you, err, 'regular'.

Boiled, roasted, mashed, chipped, pureed, juiced, souped.

History

No one is quite sure about the beginnings of the humble turnip but some people think they came from Asia or the far Northeast regions of Europe many thousands of years ago. Turnips do well in cold damp climates, so were brilliant for the poor people here in Britain. At some point in history, the turnip was replaced as an everyday vegetable by the more nutritious potato.

In 1730, Charles 'Turnip' Townshend, a British politician, imported Dutch-grown turnips to see if his livestock could survive in good health through the winter on a diet consisting of only turnips. In those days, it was expensive to grow and store hay for the whole winter, so most people killed their livestock in autumn. This meant that people had too much meat around over winter, and it was a real problem to store and keep it edible. Turnips proved to be a good way to keep livestock well-fed through harsh winters so that animals could be slaughtered as and when needed.

Turnip Trivia

- Halloween lanterns originated in the 9th century when people carved turnips to guide the souls of dead people to their former homes. We now use pumpkins.

- Mario on Game Boy Advance pulls up turnips to throw at his enemies.

- Baldrick (the fictional sidekick to Lord Blackadder) prizes turnips above all else and bought one for £400,000. Blackadder was so angry he crushed it on Baldrick's head. It happened in Black Adder the Third - Dish and Dishonesty and is well worth a watch!

- Turnips can be called 'Neeps' and are eaten with potatoes and haggis on Burns Night in Scotland.

Turnips do well in cold damp climates so they were brilliant for the poor people here in Britain. At some point in history, the turnip was replaced as an everyday vegetable by the more nutritious potato.

CELERIAC

Celeriac is a kind of celery and it is grown for its rather unattractive knobbly root which has a celery-like flavour. It is also known as celery knob, turnip rooted celery and celery root. It can be eaten raw in salads. Anything you can do with a turnip, you can do with celeriac. A lot of people think the celeriac has no place being eaten at all – it is an 'acquired taste'!

Claude Bosi, our contributing chef, uses celeriac to make jelly. He serves it with strawberries and cream. It is delicious!

WHY? Celeriac is a very underused, inexpensive vegetable so you can show off a bit by doing something tasty with it. I mean, seriously, when was the last time your mum cooked celeriac? Apart from that, celeriac is high in dietary fibre and a plentiful source of vitamins C, K + B6.

HOW... Puréed, souped, roasted, curried, boiled, mashed, jellied.

SWEDE

The swede is a cross between a cabbage and a turnip and its leaves can be eaten as a leaf vegetable. When cooked the flesh is a beautiful yellow colour. It is delicious boiled and mashed with loads of butter and served with a roast.

'Rutabaga' is the common Canadian and American name for a swede. It comes from the Swedish word Rotabagge, meaning simply 'root bag'. Swede is the preferred term used in most of the English speaking world.

Say 'Rutabaga' out loud - it is such a nice word to say! They are full of minerals including calcium and potassium. Swede is particularly low in saturated fat and high in vitamins A and C.

Baked, souped, julienned (cut into thin strips), stir fried, mashed, boiled and roasted.

Beetroot

This is an amazing vegetable! It is delicious roasted and makes wonderful chips when sliced thinly and fried in oil – yum!

Beware though that our beloved beetroot will stain absolutely everything it touches – fingers, clothes, your parents' new chopping board and that lovely new kitchen top they have just spent a fortune on. Seriously don't even try to deal with this root vegetable near anything you don't want stained a blood red colour! If the worst happens, follow these tips:

- To cure the inevitable 'pink fingers', rub with lemon juice and salt before washing with soap and water.
- On fabrics, try rubbing a slice of raw pear on the stain before washing, or rinse in cold water before washing in a biological powder.

The food industry loves this fact about beetroot and commercially uses the betanins – the natural red colourants - in beetroot to make the red in other foods even redder, such as tomato pastes, sauces, jams and even ice cream.

'Oh dear I do love you. But if you'll beetroot to me, I'll beetroot to you'

Beetroot trivia

- Since the 16th century, beet juice has been used as a natural red dye.
- Beetroot crops up in mythology and legend all over the place. Throughout history the beetroot has been all about love and is considered a love potion! It may well make you fall in love – in some cultures it is still believed that if a man and a woman eat from the same beetroot they will fall in love – but if you eat too much of it your pee and your poo turn pink! And that's not romantic at all!
- The world's heaviest beetroot weighed 23.4kg (51.48lb).
- The Lupanare – official brothel of Pompeii (the brothel still stands, despite the best efforts of Vesuvius in 79AD) – has its walls adorned with pictures of beetroots, amongst the frescoes of people having, err, fun!
- Sir Alan Sugar, of Apprentice fame, demonstrated early entrepreneurial flair when, while at school, he got a job boiling beetroots for the local greengrocer.

HISTORY

Historically it was the medicinal properties of beetroot that were more important than its eating qualities. It has been used to treat a range of ailments including fevers, constipation, wounds and various skin problems. In earlier times, the roots were long and thin like a carrot. The rounded root shape that we are familiar with today was not developed until the sixteenth century and became widely popular in Central and Eastern Europe 200 years later.

The method of pickling beetroot became very popular in England during and after World War 2, when rationing was in force and the preservation of vegetables was a nutritious, cheap and fantastic way of stocking the larder.

WHY?

Beetroot are high in magnesium and iron and so very good for your blood. They are rich in vitamins and minerals and are a great liver cleanser. Trytophan, the feel good chemical in chocolate, is present in beetroots. Note for adults - beetroot is extremely good for helping ward off the 'effects' of the night before...

HOW...

Pickled, roasted, juiced.

The Elizabethans prepared beetroot by wiping it with fresh dung before cooking it - mmm, delicious!

TOMATOES

Right, let's get this sorted right up front. Although this part of the book is about vegetables, the tomato is actually a berry therefore technically a fruit!

So why am I talking about this now? I'll tell you – because no one thinks of tomatoes as fruit and hardly anyone uses them as fruit. We use them as vegetables. The American Supreme Court sees it that way too – so who are we to argue! Anyway when was the last time your mum made a tomato crumble? Or tomato ice cream? See what I mean?

Though, actually, that sounds quite tasty. Perhaps we should give it a go...

Wow - a plethora of Vitamins including B6, C, A + K. Full of dietary fibre and loads of minerals too, notably copper and magnesium.

Raw, to get the best from these babies. Stewed as a jam, roasted, fried, stuffed and baked.

TOMATO TRIVIA

- Around the start of the 18th Century, tomatoes were used to decorate tables in some parts of Italy.

- By the mid 18th Century, tomatoes were widely eaten in Britain. In Victorian times, cultivation reached an industrial scale through the use of glasshouses.

- It is thought that the Pueblo people believed that those who witnessed other people eating tomato seeds were blessed with powers of divination – to see into the future, inspired by God.

- As tomatoes are sub-tropical, they obviously hate the cold. So why is it that your mum and dad store them in the fridge? The cold impairs ripening and inhibits their natural flavour. The best way to store them is out of all packaging and in a fruit bowl.

- Plum tomatoes were bred with a higher solid content for use in tomato sauces and pastes. They are usually oblong.

- Not all tomatoes are red. They can be yellow, orange or green.

History

Tomatoes originate from the Andes where they grew wild. They were first cultivated by the Aztecs and Incas in South America and spread all over the world following the Spanish Colonisation of the Americas. They are today the most widely grown fruit-vegetables in the world; cultivated as far north as Iceland and as far south as the Falkland Islands. Tomato seedlings have even been grown in space!

One of the earliest British cultivators of tomatoes was John Gerard. Whilst he was aware that they were happily being eaten in Spain and Italy, he believed them to be poisonous. As he was an important man, everyone listened to him and the tomato was ruled unfit for human consumption for many years.

Peppers (Capsicum)

A capsicum is a type of flowering plant which belongs to the nightshade family. They are native to South America, where they have been grown for thousands of years. When we talk of the pepper as a vegetable, we are talking about the fruit which can be red, yellow or green in colour and varies quite differently in flavour and pepperiness. They are used as vegetables, spices and medicines.

They are called peppers because of their similar flavour to the condiment black pepper but there is no botanical relationship with either that plant, or with the Sichuan pepper.

WHY? Peppers are a great source of thiamin, niacin, riboflavin and potassium. They contain lots of Vitamins A, C and E.

HOW... Raw, stir fried, grilled on the BBQ, roasted, stuffed.

History

As we said, peppers originated in South America with seeds of a wild variety dating back to 5000 BC. But how did we end up with them? Well, like many other foods native to this region, sweet peppers were carried throughout the world by the Spanish and Portuguese explorers who travelled through that continent.

Chilli peppers are perhaps the first plants to be domesticated in Central America, where there is evidence that they were consumed in 7500 BC.

Trivia

- What's the best way to cool your mouth after eating a really hot chilli pepper? Try the immediate consumption of dairy products like milk. A popular Mexican cure is to drink beer.

- The mildest peppers you can eat are bell peppers, cherry peppers and yellow peppers.

- The hottest pepper is the habanero!

- The smaller and thinner the pepper, the hotter it usually is.

And breathe...

MUSHROOMS

Mushrooms are not vegetables but since we use them in a similar way we will address them here. In fact they are not even plants and, since they are hardly animals, they needed their own classification – which they got in the 1960s. They now have their very own kingdom! In some ways, mushrooms are more closely related to animals than to plants. Just like us, mushrooms take in oxygen for their digestion and metabolism and 'exhale' carbon dioxide as a waste product.

There are many types of mushrooms and a good deal of them would kill you as soon as look at you. The general rule here is to never, ever eat anything you find in a field, stuck to the side of a tree or lurking in a damp patch. Many poisonous mushrooms look just like their non-murderous cousins and only the truly brave, madly experienced or utterly stupid would test the poison content of a mushroom by eating it.

FUNGI

Mushrooms are the fruit of some kinds of fungi, just like an apple tree will grow apples on its branches. The rest of the fungus is made up of a web of fine threads in the soil, tree or dead leaves. This 'web' of a single fungus can be huge – a honey fungus, which infects trees, once found in America was thought to be between 2,400 and 8,500 years old, and covered about 10 square kilometres of the forest.

The top of a mushroom is called the cap – inside are gills, where it produces spores, rather than seeds. Some mushrooms can release 2.7 billion spores a day, and whilst some mushrooms just drop their spores and let the wind carry them away, others shoot their spores in the air, as far as 2.5 metres.

Hieroglyphics found in the tombs of the Pharaohs suggest that the ancient Egyptians believed the mushroom to be 'the plant of immortality'. The mushroom's distinct flavour so intoxicated those demigods, that they decreed mushrooms to be food for royalty alone and prohibited any commoner from handling the delicacies.

TRUFFLES

When buying chocolates for a good friend, if money permits we might reach for the truffles. However if the shop assistant asks for several hundreds or thousands of pounds the chances are you have picked up the wrong kind of truffle. The most prized and expensive ingredient in any good kitchen will be the fungi version of the truffle.

So priceless is it that often only the head chef is allowed to touch it! A truffle is the fruit of a fungus that grows in tree roots. It is prized for its deep and rich flavour - and your pockets will also have to be deep to be able to afford one. In December 2007, a truffle sold for £195,000! That's more than the price of a family sized house in most parts of Britain!

Truffles cannot be cultivated, they must be foraged. Truffle hunters used to use pigs because of their amazing sense of smell to find these 'food diamonds' but, much to the anger of the hunters, the pigs would often eat them! Dogs are now the preferred hunter to find this priceless fungi.

The most prized truffle is the White Alba.

In 1892, the French collected around 1,000 tons of truffles every year. Today, average production is below 100 tons, hence the price.

Eaten for 4,000 years, the truffle has been described as diamond of cookery, fairy apple, black queen, gem of poor lands, fragrant nugget and black pearl.

Truffles produce a chemical almost identical to a pheromone found in male pig's saliva. As such, a female pig would be fooled into thinking she had found a boyfriend and would sniff the truffle out!

HISTORY

The word mushroom is derived from the Gallo-Roman mussiro which became mussereroun in Middle English. There is a favourite variety of Mushroom in France known as a Mousseron to this day. In the 18th century, France began cultivating mushrooms resembling the basic mushroom that we all buy at the market.

Edible mushroom species have been found inside 13,000-year-old ruins in Chile. The first reliable evidence of mushroom eating dates to several hundred years BC in China.

Mushrooms are the leading source of the essential antioxidant selenium. Antioxidants, like selenium, protect body cells from damage that might lead to chronic diseases. They also help to strengthen our immune systems. Mushrooms are low in calories, fat-free, cholesterol-free and very low in sodium, yet they provide important nutrients, including potassium, riboflavin, niacin and vitamin D. Mushrooms produce vitamin D when exposed to sunlight and UV radiation.

As well as being an excellent food source, edible mushrooms can be very good for us. They have been used in traditional Chinese medicine for thousands of years to treat many different types of health conditions, and Western scientists are now recognising the medicinal benefits of mushrooms. Don't forget, penicillin and streptomycin are examples of extremely powerful antibiotics made from fungi.

HOW... Field mushrooms are delicious stuffed with garlic and cheese. They also make a great soup. A versatile ingredient for many sauces. Sautéed, baked, deep fried.

FUNGI TRIVIA

✓ When you are told to wash and dry your feet properly 'otherwise you'll be growing mushrooms between your toes' the warning is somewhat correct. Athlete's foot is a fungus that grows between people's toes and is very itchy - around 20% of us suffer from it. So next time you are in a room with 4 other people, look around – one could be growing fungi there and then.

✓ Some mushrooms, like the stinkhorns, smell of rotting meat – that attracts flies, which then carry the spores away.

✓ Fungi that live on trees can have differing effects to that tree. Some fungi damage and kill the tree (parasitic) and others just live in the tree and help it grow (symbiotic).

✓ Some ants grow fungi for food in underground gardens.

✓ All mushrooms are fungi but not all fungi are mushrooms. The Kingdom of Fungi also includes yeasts, slime molds, rusts and several other types of related organisms.

Cabbage

Cabbage has been farmed for more than 4,000 years and has been a staple food for more than half of that time. The name 'cabbage' like many of our words comes from the French term 'caboche', which means 'head'. It was called that because the head of the cabbage is usually round. To choose a good cabbage, look for a firm compact head. Check the bottom of the stalk for signs of getting old - a dry and slightly white stalk means it was cut a while ago and is not at its freshest. There are many varieties of cabbage, which can be very different. But one common feature is that most have a short, broad stem and leaves or flowers that form a tight, compact head.

The most common cabbages are green and red cabbage, brussel sprouts and kale. The Celts brought cabbage to Europe from Asia around 600 years BC.

Broccoli

Broccoli, which has been around for more than 2000 years, is also part of the cabbage family. It is so popular that consumption has increased over 940% over the last 25 years. We think that this rise in popularity is due to the fact that a) it is lovely, and, b) it is so good for you.

Broccoli contains many vitamins and minerals, including selenium, a mineral that has been found to have anti-cancer and anti-viral properties. When choosing broccoli have a look at the stalks attached to the florets. They should be crisp so that if you break one, it will snap cleanly and easily. It shouldn't be bendy. The florets should be tightly closed and green (yellow florets mean the broccoli is old). Florets that are dark green or purplish or bluish green have more beta-carotene and vitamin C than paler florets.

What do you call two rows of leafy green vegetables?

A dual cabbage way!

CAULIFLOWER

Cauliflower, whose name means 'cabbage flower' is naturally part of the cabbage family. It is believed to have originated in the Mediterranean. Whilst the broccoli looks like little trees, the cauliflower looks a bit like a huge brain! Cauliflowers are usually white but there are unusual coloured and ornamental varieties too. The leaves around the cauliflower should be crisp and snap when you break them. Again they should not be bendy – that would mean your vegetables are old. The head of the cauliflower should be a bright white colour, if that is the variety you have bought.

Despite its health-giving properties, the cauliflower has not been treated well in literature: Mark Twain, the American author of the Huckleberry Finn and Tom Sawyer novels, once called the cauliflower 'nothing but cabbage with a college education'.

WHY?

Cabbage is a great source of vitamins A and C which your body needs for healthy skin and eyes.

Broccoli has almost double the amount of vitamin C than an orange. One cup of broccoli provides about 75 milligrams of calcium and about 1.2 milligrams of iron.

Cauliflower is high in vitamin A and is also a reasonably good source of iron.

HOW...

Cabbage - Stir fried, boiled, puréed, souped, buttered. There are other uses.

Broccoli - Roasted, mashed, steamed.

Cauliflower - Fantastic for soup, cauliflower cheese, roasted, curried.

Trivia

☑ The largest cabbage ever recorded was in 1865 and weighed 123 pounds (55.8kg). That monster of a cabbage belonged to a 19th Century farmer named William Collingwood.

☑ The Romans and Greeks thought the cabbage had great healing power. They thought it was able to cure any kind of disease or illness.

☑ In 1769, Captain Cook swore on the healing properties of the Sauerkraut, which is a fermented cabbage dish. He is said to have used the dish as a compress for the wounds of soldiers in the war. Apparently cabbage prevented the soldiers from getting infected gangrene.

Broccoli and cauliflower are examples of vegetables that are actually flowers. Don't think of getting your mum some for mother's day though - she wouldn't be impressed!

PEAS

Peas are some of the oldest known vegetables, according to the Encyclopaedia Britannica. They are so old that fossilised remains have been uncovered in Switzerland dating from the Bronze Age, as well as by archaeologists in Egyptian tombs.

It is unclear exactly where the pea originated. Some possibilities include Italy, China, Malta and Sri Lanka. In the Middle Ages, peas became popular in Europe because they were easy to grow.

The pea has many different uses. Peas are commonly fresh, frozen or tinned. Some varieties of pea pods can also be eaten such as snow peas and sugar snap peas. The sweet pea flowers are used in many body washes, soaps, lotions and perfumes. Pea shoots, from the very tip of the plant are delicious in salads.

BEANS

Beans come in many, many different varieties and are often split into two groups, 'green' and 'dry'.

Green refers to beans such as runner, French and string. That is basically when the beans themselves are too young or immature to eat, so the whole bean including the outer casing, or pod, is eaten.

Dry refers to beans such as broad, kidney and black eyed where the bean is removed from its pod and eaten.

ASPARAGUS

Asparagus comes in three colours – white, purple and green. In the UK we mostly grow the green variety and the season for that is very short, usually only from May to June. Asparagus are the young shoots from a plant which, left uncut, would grow to 150cm tall!

Peas are a good source of vitamin A, vitamin C, folate, thiamine (BI), iron and phosphorus.

Beans are loaded with proteins that your body needs and are an excellent source of carbohydrates and fibre.

Asparagus, apart from making your wee small funny, is very high in Vitamin C. It also contains collagen, which helps to keep you looking younger...

HOW...

As delicious raw as they are cooked. And only available for a short season in the late spring/summer. Take advantage and fill your boots.

AND JUST TO CONFUSE MATTERS...

Black-eyed peas are actually a variety of bean, despite their name. In the American South, eating black-eyed peas on New Year's Day is considered good luck.

Cowpea is another name for black-eyed-peas. Other names are China bean and black eyed bean. They are native to Asia and Africa, but have been cultivated since ancient times in China. Black-eyed Beans have a scented aroma, creamy texture and distinctive flavour. Those beans are characterized by their kidney shaped, white skin with a small black eye and very fine wrinkles.

BY THE WAY...

Who doesn't love beans? How many times in your life have you eaten baked beans? They are delicious and good for you. Who doesn't know this little poem?

'Beans, beans good for your heart, the more you eat the more you fart. The more you fart, the better you feel, so eat those beans at every meal'.

That poem originated from a seventeenth-century collection of graffiti on bathroom walls.

And beans will definitely make you break wind. They contain certain sugars called oligosaccharides that have a large molecular structure. That means they don't get digested very well in the small intestine, leaving lots of chunks for colonies of bacteria to eat – the bacteria produces gas as a by-product. That gas leaves your body as either a burp or a fart.

Fruits, whole grains, and some vegetables do the same thing. The bacteria in the intestines multiply when they have a lot to eat, and that process produces gas.

The gas has to come out or you would explode and that would just be wrong. Better out than in eh?

SALADS

For our purposes we will concentrate on those vegetables and leaves that you commonly see in British salads. Salads across the world vary depending on the availability of what can be grown locally.

Generally though, every salad will feature a leaf of some description. In Italy it may be rocket, a spindly, peppery leaf that looks a bit like a dandelion, whilst in the south of France it may be a crisp, sweet baby gem.

Salad comes from the Latin word 'herba salta' or 'salted herbs', so-called because such greens were usually seasoned with dressings containing lots of salt.

LETTUCE

Lettuce in Latin is lactuca, meaning milk, because often when you break the stalks a white, milk-like substance comes out. Romans revered it so highly that if a slave was caught eating one he would get whipped 30 times.

There are hundreds of lettuce varieties grown throughout the world and because they peak at different times of year there is always plenty of it. These three are the most popular:

Romaine - or Cos, long headed lettuce, most famous for its use in caesar salad.

Leaf – The epitome of summer salad. Loosely bunched leaves, dark green in colour.

Crisphead – The most common being the iceberg lettuce. Firm, compact head, holds more water content than other lettuce.

Always choose one that is crisp and free of blemishes. As with all greens, lettuce should be washed and either drained completely or blotted with a paper towel. It is possible to buy bags of prewashed lettuce, but please remember, the lettuce is washed in chlorinated water – often in a more-concentrated chlorine solution than is used than in a swimming pool. Please rewash it or, better still, buy the lettuce whole.

Lettuce is a good source of vitamin A, vitamin K and potassium. The darker the green colour of a lettuce, the higher its concentration of vitamin A.

Cucumbers, which are 90% water, contain most of the vitamins you need every day, just one cucumber contains vitamin B1, vitamin B2, vitamin B3, vitamin B5, vitamin B6, folic acid, vitamin C, calcium, iron, magnesium, phosphorus, potassium and zinc.

Cool as a cucumber...

Cucumbers

Cucumbers were thought to have originated over 10,000 years ago in southern Asia. There is some confusion over this date though, some say it was only 3,000 years ago. Either way, it's still a pretty long time.

It was very popular in the ancient civilizations of Egypt, Greece and Rome, whose people used it not only as a food but also for its beneficial skin-healing properties.

Cucumbers are scientifically known as Cucumis Sativus and belong to the same family as watermelon, pumpkin and other types of squash.

HOW...

Lettuce cannot be preserved. You can't freeze it, dry it, pickle it or can it. So eat it quickly. You can roast, or braise half heads of baby gem lettuce, however.

Varieties of cucumber are grown either to be eaten fresh or to be pickled. Those that are to be eaten fresh are commonly called slicing cucumbers. Cucumbers such as gherkins that are specially cultivated to make pickles are much smaller than slicing cucumbers.

Salad Trivia

✔ The lettuce started out as a weed around the Mediterranean basin where it has been served in dishes for more than 4500 years.

✔ The first representation of salad appeared in paintings on Egyptian tombs in 4500 BC.

✔ The ancient Greeks believed that lettuce induced sleep, so they served it at the end of the meal. The Romans continued the custom. However, the mean Emperor Domitian (81-96 AD) served it at the beginning of his feasts, so he could torture his guests by forcing them to stay awake in the presence of the Emperor.

✔ Iceberg was given its name as a result of the leaf being developed in America and being packed with ice so as to survive transportation in warm temperatures.

✔ In ancient Egypt, lettuce was sacred to the fertility god Min and considered to be a powerful aphrodisiac.

✔ The phrase 'cool as a cucumber' is not without merit. This vegetable's high water content gives it a very unique moist and cooling taste.

Cucumbers can be used to polish your shoes - not whole though!
You cut off a slice and rub it over your shoes to produce a lovely shine.

ONIONS, LEEKS & GARLIC

Onions, leeks and garlic are all in the same family. Some have a very strong pungent flavour and others in this family have a milder taste. It is hard to imagine any savoury dish without at least one of those vegetables in it.

ONIONS

Onions come in all shapes and sizes. Generally speaking the larger they are the milder the taste. We know people who eat the large, slightly sweeter, Spanish onion like an apple – hmmm.

It is believed that the onion dates back to 3500BC and originated in Asia, where the Ancient Egyptians worshipped them because they believed they symbolised eternal life.

General thinking though is that it was probably growing wild all over the world. Again what proved important to early man was how the onion kept well over the winter months. This would be why we started to cultivate them for food. There are many different types of onion - shallot, Spanish and spring onion, to name a few.

LEEKS

Leeks are delicious and provide a more subtle onion flavour to dishes such as soups. They look very different to onions but are in fact structurally pretty similar. Imagine taking an onion and stretching it into a long thin version and spraying the top half green. Leeks have multiple layers, like the onion. They can make you cry, like the onion and they taste similar to onion – when cooked they are much milder than when raw.

Leeks date back to the early Bronze Age, around 4000 BC. It is said they were part of the diet of those who built the Egyptian pyramids. And Hippocrates, the father of medicine, prescribed the leek as a cure for nosebleeds.

Garlic

Garlic is a vital ingredient to flavour many savoury dishes. The French and the Italians would literally be lost without it. Garlic is also a member of the onion family but has quite a different taste. The garlic bulb naturally comes in handy little segments and each one is packed with flavour. Many people crush garlic in a special press but some chefs will tell you it is better, if not a little tricky, to chop it into tiny pieces. Garlic burns quickly in oil and can lose its flavour if it does. The garlic flavour is deeper if added after the fast shallow frying stage. It is also delicious baked whole in the oven – taking on quite a lovely sweet taste.

What a pong!

The only real problem with garlic is that it can leave nasty bad breath after you have eaten it. At parties, in ancient Greece, the Greeks consumed so much garlic that each person got a bowl of parsley hoping it would mask their garlic breath! But don't worry if you hang around with other people who have eaten it – if you smell bad – so do they!

WHY?

Garlic allegedly gets rid of any unwanted kisses and repels Vampires. Apart from that, it is great for reinforcing your immune system. It is reported to be an antiviral, antiseptic and antibacterial. All that in one!

Onions are reputed to help to suppress the growth of potentially harmful bacteria in the colon by stimulating the growth of healthy bacteria. They also help to lower blood pressure so the next time you ask for some pocket money or an expensive game try to fill your parents full of onions first.

Nutritionally, leeks share the same benefits as both onions and garlic. They are a great source of fibre, folic acid and vitamins B6 and C. They can help improve your immune system too.

HISTORY

Garlic has been used for thousands as years and is even mentioned in the Bible. Apart from being tasty to eat, garlic is also believed to have healing powers. It was eaten by ancient Greek and Roman soldiers. Its use in China was first mentioned in AD 510.

The practice of hanging garlic, lemon and red chilli at the door or in a shop to ward off evil, is still common in India.

When the onion first arrived in Egypt it was worshipped as more than just food. Egyptians believed that it symbolized eternity – with its concentric rings. The Egyptians liked to replicate vegetables in precious metal but the onion was the only one to be glorified in gold.

During the American Civil War, General Ulysses S. Grant sent a telegram to the War Department, 'I will not move my army without onions'. The next day he got them.

Leeks have been grown since the time of the Ancient Egyptians and are still visible in tomb paintings from that period. The Romans considered the leek to be a vastly superior vegetable to others and Emperor Nero got through so many he gained the nickname Porrophagus (leek eater). He was convinced that eating leeks would give him a better singing voice!

Every Saint David's Day (1st March) you will see proud Welsh men, women and children sporting a leek. The leek is the national symbol of Wales and there are many explanations as to why. One explanation is that St. David himself ordered his soldiers to wear a leek on their helmets in a vicious battle against the detested Saxon invaders of Britain. Where did this fight take place? Apparently in a field full of leeks.

HOW...

Whole roasted bulbs of garlic are delicious. They can also be crushed into salted butter and stored in the fridge for handy garlic bread. Bulbs are also a real flavour enhancer for soups, sauces and casseroles.

Onions form the starting point for almost all sauces, stews and quiches. When gently sweated off in a pan they become less harsh and slightly sweet. Onions can also be eaten raw, pickled, roasted whole and stewed to make a fabulous French onion soup.

Leeks, once cleaned properly - a difficult process as an awful lot of earth can collect in between the layers - can be sautéed in butter, roasted, made into creamy leeks or used in pies and quiches. They cannot really be eaten raw.

DON'T CRY FOR ME...

While onions are full of flavour they are also a pain in the eyes to chop. They contain a particular oil, which has lots of sulphur in it. When you cut the onion, the oil is released. When the oil gases reach your eyes, they causes irritation and your tear glands produce tears. Whatever you do, do not rub your eyes with those hands that have been cutting the onion – ouch! There are several (somewhat odd, some of them) tricks that many people have come up with to reduce the crying and yelping…

- Hold a piece of bread in your mouth at a 90 degree angle – this will apparently 'catch' the gases before they reach your eyes!

- Wear goggles – many people swear by this.

- Peel and slice the onion under water – the onion, not you!

- Leave the root on for as long as possible – this is where most of the oil is stored – or is that an old wives tale too?

- Hold a metal teaspoon in your mouth – I think this one is just to make you look silly but it might be worth a go!

- Put lime juice on the knife blade before chopping (the acid of the lime reacts with the gas of the onion).

- Stick the onion in the freezer for 10 to 15 minutes before cutting it (it is said that chilling changes the chemical compound in the onion which causes it to release less gas).

Trivia

- According to an old English rhyme, the thickness of an onion skin can help predict the severity of the winter. Thin skins mean a mild winter is coming while thick skins indicate a rough winter.

- In Bronze Age settlements, traces of onion remains were found alongside fig and date stones dating back to 5,000 BC.

- In Ancient Greece, athletes ate large quantities of onion because it was believed that it would benefit the balance of blood.

- In the middle Ages tenants would pay their rent with onions and sometimes even give them as presents! (hmmm, must try that one...).

- The Beatles had a track called Glass Onion.

- Most onions are red, yellow or white.

- According to the Guinness Book of World Records, the largest onion ever grown weighed 10lbs 14oz (just under 5kg) and was grown in England.

- You can use an onion to clean your BBQ grill. Start by heating your grill until it is very hot – to dislodge and burn off the excess grime. Then when it is warm, rub it with half an onion to shift the rest of the grime. To then prevent everything tasting of onion, rinse it off with a salt and lemon concoction. Either that or get used to the taste of onion!

- Onions can apparently be used as an insect repellent – the only trouble is if you rub one all over your body you will repel more than just insects! According to some you can also soothe an insect bite by rubbing onion over it – onions contain an anti-inflammatory property.

- Garlic is thought to be one of the oldest foods to be cultivated. Its ability to survive a long winter out of the ground was the key to why it was so popular. It was first referenced 5000 years ago in Sanskrit, which is old Indian writing.

In Blue Hill, Nebraska, no female wearing a 'hat that would scare a timid person' can be seen eating onions in public!

Hang on a second, something doesn't seem quite right here...

Squash & Marrow

One group of vegetables that cannot be ignored is the squash or marrow family. The squash is technically a fruit – since it has seeds on the inside and therefore so are cucumbers.

Archaeological evidence suggests that squash may have been first cultivated in Mesoamerica some 8,000 to 10,000 years ago.

Summer squashes, like courgettes, pattypan and yellow crookneck are harvested during the growing season, while the skin is still soft and the fruit rather small; they are eaten almost immediately and require little-to-no cooking.

Winter squashes such as butternut and pumpkin are harvested at maturity.

In addition to the fruit, other parts of the plant are edible. Squash seeds can be eaten directly, ground into paste, meal, 'nut' butter, even a fine flour, or pressed for vegetable oil. The shoots, leaves and tendrils can be eaten as greens.

PUMPKINS

Pumpkins today are grown on six of the seven continents, with Antarctica being the sole exception. They are believed to have originated in Central America and seeds from related plants have been found in Mexico, dating back over 7000 years to 5500 BC.

Native American Indians used pumpkin as a staple in their diets centuries before the pilgrims landed. When white settlers arrived, they used pumpkins in a wide variety of recipes, from desserts to stews and soups. In addition to cooking with pumpkins, they also dried the shells and cut strips to weave into mats.

COURGETTES

Courgettes are a variety of vegetable marrow, a summer squash. They are tender and tasty when young, but most varieties are tasteless when large and overgrown. They can be eaten raw in a salad or cooked but as they are quite delicate they don't need to be cooked for long – otherwise they turn to mush.

Again they are delicious when cooked with a stronger flavour such as shallow fried in a little butter and honey. They can also be hollowed out and filled with a cooked meat mixture before being baked in the oven. The flowers are really popular to eat too. They are stuffed, cooked and served at many fine restaurants.

Butternut squash is packed full of fibre, vitamin C, magnesium, and potassium. It is also an excellent source of vitamins A and E.

Pumpkins make great Halloween lanterns and much easier to empty out than a swede or turnip. The Pumpkin is also full of many antioxidant vitamins, such as vitamins A, C and E.

Courgettes contain a high water content. They are a source of folate, potassium and vitamins A and C.

One of the best dishes of autumn is butternut or pumpkin soup. They are also delicious roasted with seasonal root vegetables. They are fabulous in a curry too and add a little sweetness.

Courgettes are best quickly sautéed in a little butter. They are a staple ingredient in ratatouille.

The original Halloween lantern is based on an 18th Century Irish folk tale and actually uses a hollowed out turnip rather than a pumpkin.

SQUASHED TRIVIA

- Of course, barely an October 31st goes by without carving a pumpkin into an ugly face and shoving a candle into it.

- Halloween evolved, in part, from the Celtic tradition of All Hallow's Eve. The famous lantern, however, came from an Irish folk tale of the 18th century. An Irishman named Jack somehow tricked the Devil into climbing into an apple tree. He then quickly cut a cross symbol in the tree trunk and trapped the Devil in the branches. When Jack died, he wasn't allowed into Heaven because of his meanness. The Devil, bearing a grudge, would not allow him into Hell. So he was forced to walk the earth alone and forever. The devil took pity on him and gave him a piece of coal to light his path. Jack put it inside a hollowed-out turnip that he had been eating.

- The smallest squash are usually the tastiest.

- The English word 'squash' derives from askutasquash (literally 'a green thing eaten raw'), a word from the Narragansett language.

- The largest pumpkin pie ever made was over five feet in diameter and weighed over 350 pounds. It used 80lb (36.2kg) of cooked pumpkin, 36lb (16.3kg) of sugar, 12 dozen eggs and took six hours to bake.

What do you get if you divide the circumference of a pumpkin by its diameter?

Pumpkin pi

VEGETABLE RECIPES

In this section...

Recipes from Claude Bosi

How tricky are the recipes? Look out for these...

Difficulty level 1

Difficulty level 2

Difficulty level 3

VEGETABLE CRISPS

Difficulty level 1

A really yummy alternative to ordinary shop bought crisps. They are delicious on their own, or served with hummus and dips.

WHAT YOU'LL NEED... (SERVES 4)

- 2 tbsp sunflower oil
- 2 carrots
- 1 sweet potato
- 2 parsnips
- Sea salt

HOW TO DO IT...

1. Wash and peel all the vegetables.

2. Finely slice the vegetables. Use a vegetable peeler or mandolin.

3. Place all the sliced vegetables into a large bowl and drizzle with the oil.

4. Using your hands, gently mix the vegetables so that they are all well coated.

5. Place on a baking sheet.

6. Bake for around 25 minutes at 200°C.

7. Give them a shuffle every five minutes.

8. Remove from the oven and put the crisps onto a wire rack.

9. When cool they will be crisp. Sprinkle with sea salt and serve.

Why not try these with hummus and other dips?

MASHED POTATOES

Learning to make the basic dishes well sets you up with loads of possibilities. From a simple mash, you can make fishcakes, hash browns, cheese pie and waffles. Your choice of potato is key, you need a good floury potato like the King Edward.

Difficulty level 1

The variety of potato that we now know as the King Edward, was introduced to the UK in 1902 by a chap called John Butler. As that coincided with the coronation of King Edward VII, the name seemed appropriate. Potatoes are one of the most important sources of vitamin C in our modern diet.

It was only after potatoes became one of our staple foods in the 18th century that scurvy began to die out! Most of us will eat a potato almost every day in one form or another, whether that's roasted, mashed, boiled, baked, jacketed and, probably the most loved, chipped.

The Mashed Potato is a dance move which was a popular dance craze of 1962.

Potatoes are only 20% solids…and 80% water.

WHAT YOU'LL NEED… (SERVES 4)

 1kg King Edwards

 250ml whole milk

 50g butter at room temperature

 Black pepper and sea salt

HOW TO DO IT…

1. Peel potatoes and cut into pieces roughly the same size. The smaller you chop them the quicker they will cook through – so you decide. Usually, pieces the size of an Oxo cube are good.

2. Put spuds in a medium saucepan and add just enough water cover them, not too much. Switch on the heat and bring to the boil. Add a pinch of salt. Simmer for 15 minutes.

3. Poke with a knife, if it slides off easily then it is ready, if there is still some resistance then cook for a few more minutes.

4. Drain into a colander and leave for a few minutes, this allows a lot of steam to evaporate so the potatoes are not too watery. Place back in your empty, dry but unwashed saucepan.

5. Throw in the chopped butter and start mashing. Season with salt and pepper to your taste. Don't forget if you are using salted butter you will need less salt – always taste to check the seasoning.

Make sure you butter the toast whilst it's warm, to ensure it's lovely and melted.

Difficulty level 1

Garlic Mushrooms on Toast

What you'll need... (Serves 2)

- 250g button mushrooms or big beef mushrooms sliced
- 2 cloves garlic, crushed
- A good handful of chopped fresh tarragon
- 150ml double cream
- Thick sliced wholemeal bread, toasted and spread with butter
- 1 tablespoon olive oil
- 1 tablespoon of salted butter
- 50g grated parmesan

How to do it...

1. Fry the mushrooms on a medium heat in the butter and olive oil.

2. Add the garlic and a good handful of finely chopped tarragon. Cook for a minute or two – stirring all the time then stir in the cream. Add the parmesan cheese.

3. Turn up the heat and warm through. The sauce should be lovely thick and creamy.

4. Serve piping hot on warm buttered toast.

CRISPY VEGETABLE FINGERS

Difficulty level 1

At a glance you'd think these were fish fingers. As this is the veggie section they're obviously not - but they're just as yummy.

WHAT YOU'LL NEED... (SERVES 4)

- Half head broccoli, steamed until soft then broken into small pieces with a fork
- 1 potato, baked, centre scooped out and mashed with a little butter
- 1 carrot, grated
- 1 shallot, finely chopped
- Dried breadcrumbs
- 1 egg
- 1 teaspoon baking powder
- 50g grated cheddar cheese

HOW TO DO IT...

1. While you are heating your oven to 180°C place all your ingredients into a large bowl and mix well.

2. Take a small amount of the mixture between your hands and roll into a sausage shape.

3. Place on baking parchment paper on a baking sheet and flatten your 'sausages' slightly with a fork. This will give the finished product a pleasing ridge across the top.

4. Bake the vegetable fingers for 20-25 minutes, flipping them over after 10 minutes. Serve straight away with a good salad.

5. This dish can be prepared a day in advance of cooking and left to chill overnight before cooking.

Mushy Peas with Fresh Mint

Difficulty level 1

What can we say about mushy peas? Love them or not, they are a firm favourite in the UK. Where would fish and chips be without the required dollop of greying green sidekick?

Mushy peas are dried marrowfat peas. They are first soaked overnight in water and then simmered with a little sugar and salt.

So what constitutes a marrowfat pea? Simply put they are mature peas. Instead of being harvested young to be frozen immediately or sold as fresh they are left out in the field to dry naturally.

In Ireland, marrowfat peas are considered a delicacy and are often served on Sundays at family dinners, especially in the Galway region. Some people believe those peas played an important role in the process of Ireland becoming independent again. Nowadays they are one of the main ingredients for wedding meals on Ireland's west coast. It is said that the more marrowfat is eaten during the wedding ceremony, the happier the couple will be during the first 7 years of their marriage.

What You'll Need... (Serves 4)

 250g dried marrowfat peas

 Salt and pepper

 2 teaspoon bicarbonate of soda

 Chopped fresh mint leaves

How to do it...

1. Place the peas in a large bowl – the peas will swell as they absorb liquid and so need plenty of room. Add the bicarbonate of soda and cover with 850ml boiling water. Stir and leave overnight to soak.

2. After their long over-night soak, drain and place in a saucepan. Cover with cold water.

3. Bring to the boil and cook until mushy. This will take about 30 minutes. Taste and decide whether salt and pepper need to be added.

4. Add the chopped mint leaves, stir and serve immediately.

5. Any leftovers can be blended. With the addition of a little water or milk and a little single cream, they will make a fabulous soup.

Basic Summer Salad

Difficulty level 1

Remember to drizzle the dressing over the salad just before you serve

How many times have you been given a dull lifeless salad. And then, to make things even worse, you're moaned at when you push it around the plate. Truth is, we take great care in preparing hot food yet often with salad we just simply chop it up and consider it ready to eat. Fresh vegetables are delicious raw and untreated, don't get me wrong, but as a plate of food they can be underwhelming.

Preparing a salad is cooking, if you do it properly. For example you should add the onions to the dressing first and leave for 15 minutes. The vinegar in the dressing actually cooks the onion and removes some of the harshness, leaving you with a softer, more subtle flavour.

What you'll need… (Serves 4)

- ✓ 1 tablespoon of balsamic vinegar
- ✓ 1 sliced red onion
- ✓ 2 sliced, washed and dried baby gem lettuce.
- ✓ 3 tablespoon olive oil
- ✓ 1 sliced tomato

How to do it…

1. Mix the balsamic vinegar with the oil in a large bowl then add the onion and cover. Leave for 15 minutes to soften.

2. Lay the tomatoes on top and then drop in the baby gem lettuce.

3. With your hands mix all the ingredients together, but only JUST before you are ready to serve. Otherwise the tomatoes will go mushy and the baby gem will discolour.

4. This is a basic salad, you can also put in many other ingredients such as apple, grapes or a hard-boiled egg, in fact any flavour you fancy. Go wild and experiment as you wish, but by starting with this basic salad, you cannot really go wrong.

For extra sweetness try adding
mango chutney to the sauce

VEGETABLE MASALA

You've probably heard of chicken tikka masala. The tikka (chunks of chicken marinated in spices) served in a rich-tasting red/orange sauce (masala). The sauce is usually creamy, lightly spiced and contains tomatoes. It is reported that chicken tikka masala is now the most popular takeaway dish in Britain and it has been labelled 'a true British national dish'.

Difficulty level 1

The origins of chicken tikka masala are not clear. One expert on street food insists that it was created in Punjab during within the last 50 years. Another view is that it originated in the first Indian restaurants in Soho, London, during the 1970s.

Our masala dish uses no meat. Instead it uses up pretty much any and all of the root vegetables in the bottom drawer of your fridge. It is tasty and healthy and you can add in masses of flavour into otherwise bland vegetables.

What you'll need... (Serves 4)

- ✅ Half head broccoli
- ✅ 1 sweet potato
- ✅ Half of an under-ripe mango
- ✅ 1 tin coconut milk
- ✅ Knob of butter

- ✅ Half head cauliflower
- ✅ 2 large onions
- ✅ Olive oil
- ✅ 3 tablespoons masala paste
- ✅ Handful of mange tout, thinly sliced carrot, French beans

How to do it...

1. Dice the onions and cook in a shallow pan with a drizzle of olive oil until tender. Take the onions out of the pan with a slotted spoon and set aside on a plate.

2. Now peel and chop the sweet potato into approximately 2cm cubes. Sweet potatoes are much denser than ordinary potatoes and much tougher to cut.

3. In the same unwashed pan, add a knob of butter and melt over a medium heat then add the sweet potatoes. Cover and cook until browned and a little softer. Remember they are dense so will not be cooked all the way through. Add the onions back to the sweet potato.

4. Add the masala paste to a separate saucepan and warm through. Cook for 2 minutes and then add the whole tin of coconut milk.

5. When the masala sauce comes to the boil add the sweet potato and onion mixture to it.

6. Continue to simmer until the potatoes are almost cooked through.

7. Add the rest of the vegetables in order of size, cauliflower and broccoli first, beans and smaller vegetables after.

8. Check the thickest part of the broccoli or cauliflower stalk by poking it with a sharp knife. When it is soft, the curry is cooked.

9. Before serving add small slices of the mango, which adds a little sweetness to the dish, or a good dollop of mango chutney – or both. The curry is yours, so tweak it to suit your taste.

10. Serve with rice or Indian style flat bread.

Scrummy by itself, with a jacket potato or as a side dish!

Cauliflower Cheese with Golden Raisins & Curry

Difficulty level 1

Cauliflower cheese is a traditional British dish made with British cauliflowers, which are available almost all year round. This recipe has an unusual twist with the addition of raisins and curry powder. A cauliflower cheese recipe is so easy, and versatile – you could add all kinds of other ingredients, ham, tuna, tomato – whatever you fancy.

The standard cauliflower cheese appears throughout British food in many different ways; a side dish at Sunday lunch, a tasty filling for jacket potatoes and sometimes, even as the filling for a pasty or quiche. Cauliflower cheese can also be blended and, with a little extra milk added, makes a delicious and wholesome soup.

What you'll need... (Serves 4)

- 1 medium cauliflower
- 55g butter
- 55g all plain flour
- Large pinch salt
- 1 pint milk

- 75g cheddar cheese, grated plus extra for sprinkling on top
- Black pepper
- Small handful golden raisins
- 1 tablespoon medium curry powder

How to do it...

1. Preheat the oven to 200°C.

2. Remove the green outer leaves from the cauliflower.

3. Chop into florets all approximately the same size.

4. Bring a saucepan of salted water to the boil, add the cauliflower.

5. Boil until the base of the cauliflower floret is beginning to go soft.

6. Drain and allow to steam dry for a while.

7. You now need to make the sauce, using a basic roux technique.

8. Place the butter and flour into a large saucepan. Over a low heat stir the butter and flour until the butter has melted and the flour is incorporated.

9. Add the salt and curry powder and continue stirring for 2 minutes until it becomes a thick paste.

10. Turn the heat off and add a little of the milk to the paste. Stir until the paste is a little thinner. Add more milk and do the same over and over until the paste has a thinner consistency.

11. Add the rest of the milk and turn the heat back on and bring to the simmer, stirring all the time. You will end up with a smooth sauce. Continue stirring until the sauce is thickened and glossy, which should take about 5 minutes. If your roux seems a little lumpy when you add the milk, use a metal whisk. This will get rid of the lumps of flour

12. If the sauce is very thick add a little more milk. The sauce should be thick but still runny, a little bit like custard. Add the cheese and stir until melted. Remove from the heat.

13. Place the florets in a baking dish large enough to hold all the florets in one layer. Sprinkle the golden raisins over the top.

14. Pour the thickened cheese sauce over the cauliflower ensuring all the florets are covered.

15. Sprinkle with grated cheese and a good twist of black pepper.

16. Bake in the hot oven until the sauce is bubbling and golden brown on the top.

17. Don't forget everything is already cooked so this is just a browning exercise and shouldn't take long.

ROAST WINTER VEGETABLES WITH THYME

Difficulty level 2

This is lovely as a dish all on its own, or as a side dish. It really is winter on a plate. I find it nutritious and warming, it's real feel-good food.

If you want to make this dish on its own, try adding a fried egg on top and maybe add some cooked sausages.

WHAT YOU'LL NEED… (SERVES 2, OR 4 AS A SIDE DISH)

- 2 large cloves garlic, peeled and crushed
- 12 shallots, peeled
- 1 peeled and de-seeded butternut squash
- 2 large sweet potatoes
- 1 peeled swede
- Half head of peeled celeriac
- 2 sprigs thyme
- 3 tablespoons olive oil
- Salt & black pepper

HOW TO DO IT…

1. This dish is easy. Cut the vegetables into large, even, chunky pieces and place into a bowl.

2. Add the garlic, olive oil and lots of seasoning and use your hands to mix them.

3. Spread on to a baking tray, drizzle a little more oil, throw on the thyme.

4. Bake at 200°C for 45 minutes until all the vegetables are soft and caramelised.

Sweet Broad Bean Patties

This recipe dates back to the Saxon times when food would have been cooked on a hanging griddle near an open fire. The cakes are best eaten hot but are also good cold. They are delicious with a slice of cheese or a real treat with a dollop of good ice cream.

The broad bean plant is one of the most ancient plants in cultivation. Along with lentils, peas, and chickpeas, broad beans became part of the eastern Mediterranean diet or around 6000 BC. If you suffer with warts it is worth knowing this old folk remedy that, when rubbed, the velvet insides of the broad bean pods cure them! In many Arab countries, the broad bean is eaten for breakfast. In Italy, broad beans are traditionally sown on November 2nd, All Souls Day.

What You'll Need... (Serves 4)

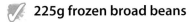 225g frozen broad beans

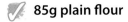 85g plain flour

 100ml milk (approx)

 2 dessert spoonfuls clear honey

 Knob of butter

(You don't have to serve it on a log by the way)

How to Do It...

1. Defrost the beans and, when defrosted, chop roughly. Add the flour and then add the milk to make a paste.

2. Add the runny honey. The batter needs to be of a consistency that drops off your spoon, so add a little more milk if it is too thick.

3. When the batter will drop from the spoon, lightly grease a frying pan with butter.

4. When bubbling, drop little spoonfuls of the bean batter into the pan.

5. Reduce the heat so the patties cook through. You will need to turn them a few times so they don't burn.

6. When golden on both sides they are ready. Try with marmalade for a delicious treat!

Coleslaw

Difficulty level 2

Sometimes simply called 'slaw' in America, coleslaw is a type of salad consisting of shredded raw cabbage & carrots. The name 'coleslaw' came about in the 20th century as an English variation of the Dutch term 'koolsla', a shortening of 'koolsalade', which means 'cabbage salad'.

Usually served as a side dish or sandwich filler you can create many different variations on the original. Broccoli-slaw is made replacing the cabbage with raw broccoli. You could also add cheese, pineapple or ham.

What you'll need... (Serves 4)

- 30ml mayonnaise
- 1ml lemon juice
- 150g natural yogurt
- Salt & pepper
- 225g white cabbage, very finely shredded
- 225g red cabbage, very finely shredded
- 1 eating apple, unpeeled, cored and cut into matchstick strips
- 50g sultanas

How to do the dressing...

1. Put the mayonnaise and lemon juice in a bowl, whisk until smooth.

2. Slowly beat in the yoghurt and season to taste.

How to do the salad...

1. Put the cabbages, apple and sultanas in a large bowl. Pour over the dressing and toss together until well coated in the dressing.

2. Cover and chill until ready to serve. Use as an accompaniment to a BBQ or as a side dish for a lovely plate of spare ribs.

You can create lots of variations with your coleslaw by adding extra elements, such as slices of apple.

Delicious as part of a cooked breakfast too.

RATATOUILLE
– NOT JUST A FILM…

Difficulty level 2

Pronounced 'Rat at too ii'.

A traditional French Provençal stewed vegetable dish, the name ratatouille comes from an old version of the French language known as Occitan. Occitan was at one point in time spoken fluently by over half of the French population and is still spoken widely in Catalonia today. The French touiller means to toss food. Ratatouille originates from the areas we know nowadays as Nice and Provence.

The 2007 film of the same name depicts Remy, a rat, who dreams of becoming a great French chef. So he arrives in Paris only to find out that his cooking idol is dead. When he makes an unusual alliance with a restaurant's new garbage boy, the culinary and personal adventures begin, despite Remy's family's scepticism and the rat-hating world of humans.

WHAT YOU'LL NEED… (SERVES 4)

- 2 large aubergines
- 4 small courgettes
- 2 red peppers
- 4 large tomatoes
- 5 tablespoons olive oil
- Small bunch basil leaves

- 1 medium onion, peeled and thinly sliced
- 3 garlic clove, peeled and crushed
- 1 tablespoon red wine vinegar
- 1 teaspoon sugar

How to do it...

1. First salt your aubergines to draw out the bitterness and firm the flesh. To do this, slice them thickly lengthwise and sprinkle the cut surfaces with salt - ½ teaspoon is sufficient for 450g of aubergines.

2. Place the salted flesh in a colander or sieve and let it stand for about 30 minutes.

3. Rinse the flesh, squeeze out the excess moisture and pat dry with paper towels. Cut into 2cm chunks.

4. Cut off the courgettes ends, then slice across to create circles about 1 ½cms thick.

5. Peel the peppers and cut into similar sized pieces.

6. Score a small cross on the base of each tomato and put them into a heatproof bowl.

7. Pour boiling water over the tomatoes, leave for 20 seconds and then drop the tomatoes into icy cold water. Leave to cool and then peel the now loose skin away. Roughly chop the tomatoes and keep in a separate dish.

8. Put a pan over medium heat and, when hot, pour in 2 tablespoons of olive oil.

9. Brown the aubergines for 5 minutes on each side or until the pieces are soft. Take them out of the pan with a slotted spoon and put them to one side on a plate.

10. Then fry the courgettes in another tablespoon of olive oil (in the now empty pan) for 5 minutes or until golden on both sides. Remove these from the pan and repeat the process with the peppers.

11. Using your hands, tear up the basil leaves and set aside.

12. Cook the onion in the pan for 5 minutes and add the garlic - fry for a further minute.

13. Stir in the vinegar and sugar and then tip in the tomatoes and the basil.

14. Return all your cooked vegetables back to the pan with some salt and pepper and continue to cook for 10 minutes. Serve either as a whole dish or as an accompaniment to a Sunday roast or as part of a huge cooked breakfast.

Ratatouille is fab eaten hot but you could try eating it cold. Also try warmed up with a freshly poached egg on top. Leftovers can be used as a great pizza topping.

Spanish Potato Omelette

Difficulty level 2

Let's get the name right first, tortilla de patatas, tortilla española or Spanish omelette is a typical Spanish dish which is an egg omelette with fried potatoes. It also includes onion, depending on the region of Spain that the particular version comes from.

One of the most common tapas throughout Spain and a firm favourite at Spanish picnics, tortilla can be enjoyed hot or cold.

What you'll need... (Serves 4)

- 300g of potato (any type except new potatoes)
- 5 medium eggs
- ½ medium white onion
- Olive oil
- Salt
- Black pepper

Why not try other ingredients, such as ham or tomato, in your omelette?

How to do it...

1. Peel the potatoes, cut in half and slice thinly.

2. Scatter salt over the sliced potatoes.

3. Finely chop the half onion.

4. Add two tablespoons of olive oil to a frying pan, then warm over a medium heat.

5. When hot, add the potatoes. Keep turning and separating them for 5 minutes. If they start to turn a deep brown, lower the heat. Do not crisp them.

6. Add the chopped onions and mix in well. Cover the frying pan and turn the heat very low and allow the potatoes to sweat under the lid.

7. Break the eggs into a large bowl. Whisk them with a fork but only enough to mix the whites and yolks together. Add salt and pepper.

8. When the potatoes and onions are cooked, add them to the bowl of eggs.

9. In the same frying pan add a drizzle of olive oil. Turn up the heat to medium.

10. Pour the bowl of eggs and potato into the pan and then turn down the heat to the lowest setting. Leave the omelette to cook for 15 minutes at the lowest heat setting.

11. When there is almost no liquid on the surface of the omelette and it is almost completely set, flip it over. If you are not confident to do it with a flick then try taking the pan off the heat and place a large dinner plate over the omelette. The plate should be large enough to cover the whole pan. Tip the pan upside down with the omelette dropping onto the plate. Then put the pan back on the hob and slide the omelette back into the pan with the cooked side facing up.

12. Turn the heat back up and gently cook the other side. This won't take long at all – about a minute. Then turn out and serve with a fresh salad.

This is a traditional recipe. You can add other ingredients such as peppers, tomatoes, cheese or ham.

Pumpkin Spaghetti Cakes with Aged Parmesan

Difficulty level 2

For this recipe, we are using a variety of pumpkin known as the spaghetti pumpkin. Its flesh is bright yellow, orange or white. When raw, the flesh is solid and similar to other raw squash; when cooked, the flesh falls away from the fruit in ribbons or strands like spaghetti.

What you'll need... (Serves 5)

- 1 spaghetti pumpkin
- 2 diced shallots
- Olive oil
- Vegetable oil for frying
- 100g grated fresh parmesan cheese
- Some plain flour
- 1 egg

How to do it...

1. Cut the pumpkin in half and pull all the seeds out with your hands.

2. Carefully scoop out the inside with a spoon.

3. Place the pumpkin spaghetti to one side.

4. Take a frying pan and heat with a drizzle of olive oil.

5. Add the shallots. Cook them until they are golden brown and sticky – in other words caramelise them. Set aside and cool.

6. In a mixing bowl, add the egg, pumpkin, parmesan and shallots and mix well.

7. With your hands make 10 small balls of the mixture and flatten in to small rounds. Then roll them in the flour to give them a light coating. The egg will help the flour to stick.

8. Pop into a frying pan with a little hot vegetable oil and cook until golden brown in colour.

9. Serve piping hot with salads.

BUBBLE AND SQUEAK BURGER

Difficulty level 2

This dish empties your fridge of leftovers and is very tasty, nutritious and versatile. Bubble and Squeak is Cockney rhyming slang for Greek

These burgers are perfect served with a simple minted yoghurt. We cheat by adding 1 teaspoon of mint sauce to 1 cup natural yoghurt.

WHAT YOU'LL NEED... (SERVES 4)

- 450g of evenly sliced potato
- 55g green cabbage
- 55g mature cheddar, grated
- 1 tablespoon plain flour
- 1oz salted butter, melted
- 1 dessert spoon olive oil
- Salt and pepper

HOW TO DO IT...

1. Boil potatoes until they are soft, close to the mash-able texture you obtained in the best mash recipe.

2. When almost cooked, throw in the cabbage and cook for a further two minutes.

3. Drain and let some of the steam evaporate. Whilst warm, season with salt and pepper. Add a handful of grated cheese.

4. Mix well, the potato will mash during this process.

5. Separate into 8 balls and flatten with your hands.

6. Squish and dust each burger lightly with flour.

7. Preheat oven to 220°C.

8. Brush both sides of the burger with olive oil and melted butter.

9. Place on a hot baking tray and return to the hot shelf for 15 minutes.

10. Serve as a snack or as an accompaniment to a roast dinner. It also makes an excellent breakfast.

For extra warmth try grinding some black pepper over the top

BUTTERNUT SQUASH SOUP
TOASTED HAZELNUTS & OLIVE OIL

Difficulty level 2

Characterised by its yellow skin and orange fleshy pulp the butternut squash turns increasingly deep orange, and becomes sweeter and richer. Popular in South Africa and known as butternut pumpkin in the USA this vegetable is packed full of fibre, magnesium and potassium. It is also an excellent source of vitamins A, C & E.

WHAT YOU'LL NEED... (SERVES 4)

- 1 large butternut squash, peeled, seeded and diced into small cubes
- 2 diced shallots
- 50g whole hazelnuts, out of their shells
- Sprig of thyme
- Dusting icing sugar
- Good quality olive oil
- 300ml of single cream

HOW TO DO IT...

1. Put a saucepan on a moderate heat with a dessert spoon of olive oil and diced shallots.

2. When the shallots are tender, but not brown, add the butternut squash and the thyme.

3. Mix together and cover with a lid, turn down the heat.

4. Stir occasionally to make sure the squash doesn't stick.

5. Let all the condensation that accrues on the lid fall into the pan. This adds liquid to the soup.

6. Cook until all the squash is really mushy. Remove from heat.

7. Place the hazelnuts on a baking tray and sprinkle them lightly with icing sugar.

8. Pop them under a hot grill and allow them to caramelise, they should be a nice golden colour. Keep an eye on them – the high oil content in nuts mean they can burn very quickly!

9. Empty onto a cold plate and leave them to cool a little before carefully crushing.

10. Remove the thyme sprig from the squash and throw it away.

11. Pour the squash into a liquidiser, put on the lid and blend to a smooth consistency.

12. Put your soup back into a pan and warm it back up.

13. Add the pot of single cream, stir well.

14. When hot, ladle the soup into bowls, sprinkle with a few hazelnuts and drizzle a really small amount of olive oil on top.

15. If your soup appears too thick at this point you can add a little water from the kettle to thin it. It should, however, have a thick and creamy texture.

16. Serve with big hunks of soft white bread.

Moussaka

Difficulty level 3

A dish of Greek origins, the moussaka usually has minced lamb in the recipe. However, it can be equally delicious without. The moussaka always has aubergine in the recipe. Different varieties of aubergine plant produce fruits of different sizes, shape and colour, though typically purple. There are even orange varieties. The aubergine plants originally came from India and in America the aubergine is known as eggplant.

What you'll need... (Serves 4)

- ✅ **500g potatoes**
- ✅ **2 courgettes**
- ✅ **3 aubergines**
- ✅ **Olive oil**
- ✅ **Salt**
- ✅ **Black pepper**

& for the Sauce...

- ✅ **500g chopped button mushrooms**
- ✅ **1 crushed garlic clove**
- ✅ **1 tin chopped tomatoes**
- ✅ **1 medium onion finely sliced**
- ✅ **1 tablespoon chopped parsley**
- ✅ **Olive oil**

& for the Béchamel...

- ✅ **500ml fresh milk**
- ✅ **125g butter**
- ✅ **100g grated parmesan cheese**
- ✅ **60g plain flour**

How to do it...

1. First salt, or de-gorge, your aubergines to draw out the bitterness and firm the flesh. Slice them up lengthwise and sprinkle the cut surfaces generously with salt. Place the salted flesh in a colander or sieve and let it stand for about 30 minutes.

2. Rinse the flesh, squeeze out the excess moisture, and pat dry with paper towels.

3. Slice the potatoes and courgettes lengthwise into ½cm slices. Place the sliced potatoes on a baking tray, drizzle with olive oil, season with salt and pepper.

4. Place in a hot oven and cook until light golden. Repeat this process with both the aubergine and the courgette. Remove from the oven and allow to cool.

Don't be afraid of crispy bits like this, they're delicious!

MUSHROOM SAUCE

5. Gently fry the onions and garlic in a large pan. Add the mushrooms and sauté until all the juices have evaporated. Add the tomatoes and then the parsley. Continue cooking until you have a thick sauce.

BÉCHAMEL SAUCE

6. Place the butter into a large saucepan and allow to melt, but not bubble. Add the flour and mix to a paste. Add the milk a little at a time, stirring continuously. If it becomes lumpy, use a whisk to mix.

7. Once all the milk has been added, mix your cheese into the sauce well. Season with salt and pepper.

ASSEMBLY

8. Take a deep oven dish and line the bottom with a layer of cooked potato. Then add a layer of the courgettes followed by a layer of aubergine.

9. Spread the mushroom sauce on top.

10. Add a final layer with the remaining potatoes on top of the tomato sauce. Carefully spread the béchamel sauce over and bake in an oven at 180°C for approximately 45 minutes or until it has turned a golden colour on top. If you want you can add a sprinkle of cheese on top of the white sauce.

Risotto with Spring Vegetables

Difficulty level 3

Notorious for being difficult to make, risotto actually isn't. This version uses a variety of rice known as Arborio, an Italian short-grain rice named after the town of Arborio in the Po Valley, where it is grown. Arborio rice has a higher starch content than other varieties of rice and is therefore chewier and ideal for dishes such as risotto and rice pudding.

What you'll need... (Serves 4)

- 225g Arborio rice
- 1 medium onion, peeled and sliced
- 150ml white wine
- 550ml vegetable stock
- 1 tbsp olive oil
- 50g salted butter
- Fresh grated parmesan
- 12 green asparagus spears
- Handful broad beans
- Handful peas
- 2 tablespoons pesto

How to do it...

1. Heat the olive oil in a saucepan, add the onion and cook until soft.

2. Add the rice and continue to cook without colouring it.

3. Season, with salt and pepper. Add the wine and bring immediately to the boil. Let the wine reduce completely then add half the vegetable stock. Bring back to the boil. Then take of the heat. Allow to cool, as it does so, the rice will absorb the stock.

4. 15 minutes before you are ready to eat pour the rest of the stock onto the rice. Bring back to the boil and add butter and approximately 25g of parmesan cheese. Leave to simmer. The risotto will be perfect when all the stock has been absorbed. It should have just a little 'bite', which gives it an al dente texture.

5. Stir in the pesto. Season with salt and pepper.

6. Bring some salted water to the boil and cook your vegetables in order of size: asparagus first, then add broad beans, then peas. Make sure they are not over cooked; they should be al dente, so they are still crispy and crunchy. Drain off the water, season with salt, pepper and a little oil. Stir the cooked vegetables into the risotto. Spoon the vegetable risotto onto warmed plates and sprinkle with parmesan cheese. Serve immediately.

STUFFED SPANISH ONIONS

Difficulty level 3

It has been reported that bulbs from the onion family have been used as a food source for millennia. In Bronze Age settlements, traces of onion remains were found alongside fig and date stones dating back to 5000 BC. The Ancient Egyptians worshipped onions believing that they symbolised eternal life. Most onions are red, yellow or white. Texts from India dated to the early 6th Century describe how onions were used as medicine. They were taken for the heart, the eyes and the joints.

WHAT YOU'LL NEED… (SERVES 4)

- ✓ 4 medium Spanish onions peeled but left whole
- ✓ 150g baby spinach
- ✓ 250g ricotta cheese
- ✓ 1 egg yolk
- ✓ 1 tsp nutmeg, freshly grated
- ✓ 100g parmesan, freshly grated
- ✓ 15g butter

HOW TO DO IT…

1. Bring a pan of salted water to the boil. Add the whole, peeled onions and boil for 5 minutes, drain and set aside to cool.

2. Wash the spinach and place in a saucepan. Cover and cook the spinach for 3-4 minutes until wilted. Allow to cool then press in a clean teatowel to dry and chop roughly.

3. In a mixing bowl mix together the ricotta, spinach, egg yolk, nutmeg and 75g of the parmesan cheese. Season to taste with salt and black pepper.

4. When the onions are cool slice the tops off (approx. 1cm down). Take out the middle of the onion with a small fork. Stuff the hollowed out onions with the ricotta mixture.

5. Put the onions in a small roasting tin, sprinkle over the remaining Parmesan and dot with the butter. Roast for 30 minutes at 200°C until the cheese is bubbling and golden brown. Serve.

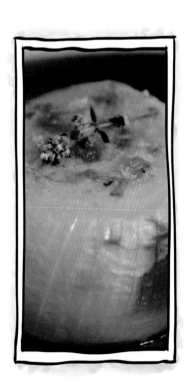

Why not use the carrot tops for decoration?

CARROT CAKE

Carrots have been used in sweet cakes since the medieval period as they contain more sugar than any other vegetable besides sugar beet. They were also easy to find and were cheap - other sweeteners were very expensive and rare back then. The origins of carrot cake are unknown, but it is said to come from Sweden. In World War 2 Britain, with rationing prevalent, the cake became very popular.

Difficulty level 3

In America, carrot cakes first became popular in the early 1960s. In 2005, the American-based Food Network listed carrot cake, with its cream-cheese icing, as number five of the top food favourites of the 1970s. Move over prawn cocktail. Carrot cake can also be known as passion cake.

WHAT YOU'LL NEED FOR THE ICING...

 200g cream cheese

 4 level tbsp icing sugar

 Few drops vanilla extract

& FOR THE CAKE... (SERVES 6)

- 175g self-raising flour
- 1 level tsp baking powder
- 2 level tsp ground mixed spice
- 3 medium eggs
- 150ml sunflower oil
- 175g soft light brown sugar
- 100g raisins
- 250g carrots, peeled and grated
- Pinch of salt

HOW TO DO IT...

1. Tip the flour into a bowl and stir in the baking powder, spice and salt.

2. Then stir in all the remaining cake ingredients until well mixed.

3. Pour the mixture into a 1kg tin, buttered and lined.

4. Bake in centre of preheated oven at 180°C, it will take about 60 minutes.

5. To check the cake is baked, push a metal skewer into the centre. It should come out clean with no sticky cake mixture stuck to it. The cake should also be just firm to the touch in the centre.

6. Remove from the oven, allow to cool for 15 minutes, then turn the cake out onto a wire rack. Allow to cool.

7. Mix together the cream cheese, vanilla extract and icing sugar.

8. Spread evenly over the top surface of the carrot cake, leave to set. Serve.

A VARIATION OF THIS RECIPE...

By changing these few ingredients below, you will make a really interesting and tasty version. This recipe does not require icing. The consistency of the finished cake will be doughier and more moist than the carrot cake, and is amazing served just warm with clotted cream.

1. Replace the 250g of carrots with 250g of grated butternut squash.

2. Replace the vegetable oil with 150ml of olive oil.

3. Also add zest of 1 whole orange.

4. Throw in a good handful of chopped dark cooking chocolate.

5. Add 1 teaspoon of marmalade.

Interior of Hibiscus restaurant

Recipes from Claude Bosi

Just off Regent Street, in London's busy Mayfair, on a small thoroughfare called Maddox Street lies Hibiscus restaurant. Blink and you will miss it, for it's a very discreet entrance. Enter and you will see a small, pale, oak-panelled dining room with a polished wooden floor and only 14 tables.

Claude Bosi was born and raised in Lyon, in the Rhone Valley, southeast France. The eldest son of the owners of a typical French bistro, Claude was thrown out of his mothers' kitchen at an early age. He had set fire to the place by pouring water into a pan frying eggs. The fire exploded, as did the tempers of Claude's parents. So at the tender age of just 14 Claude was taken to the famous restaurant the Leon de Lyon to begin his 'apprentissage', or work placement.

More than 20 years on and Claude's career has seen him work at some of the toughest kitchens in the gastronomic country of France; enduring long hours, low pay and temperamental chefs. His career in the UK has seen him move his beloved restaurant Hibiscus from the bustling market town of Ludlow, Shropshire, to Mayfair, London. But his love for raw ingredients and the art of cooking has stayed with him throughout and he is now internationally acclaimed as one of the best chefs in the world.

Although a double Michelin-starred chef with many accolades under his belt, Claude also loves to cook simple food at home for family and friends.

A FEW WORDS FROM
CLAUDE BOSI
Chef / Patron of Hibiscus Restaurant, Mayfair.

Vegetables. We are supposed to have 5 portions of vegetables and fruit a day. We fight like crazy to get our children to eat them. We tend gardens, slay slugs and frantically erect bits of wire and netting to lovingly protect our crops. We include them in a balanced diet and even disguise them in various ways. But do we explain where they come from? Do we offer anything children other than 'they're good for you' as a reason to eat them?

Young people have quick, intelligent and versatile minds. I believe to capture the interest of those minds, you have to stimulate them. That is exactly what this book does. I also believe that many adults will find Villainous Vegetables a hard one to put down.

Both Petrie and Claire write with enthusiasm and light-heartedness and manage to connect with the reader, no matter what their age. Their relaxed and humorous style of writing combined with manageable, yet interesting recipes makes this not only a great cook book, but also an enjoyable read.

The majority of the great chefs of the world, those at the top of their game, all share a common fact. They learned to cook when young. Those chefs have loved food since childhood and that influences their adult lives and careers. They all share a passion for not only the cooked dish, but for raw ingredients. They are still keen to learn and they are open to new experiences. Food has history, as we said. But it is still evolving. We can never learn everything there is to know because it keeps changing.

The message is simple. Get in the kitchen, kids, and get cooking.

Claude Bosi

Beetroot and Orange Tart with Iced Feta Cheese

Difficulty level 3

What you'll need... (Serves 6)

- 900g feta cheese
- 1 leaf gelatine
- 400g sugar syrup
- 6 red beetroot
- 2 large oranges
- Shop bought puff pastry
- Icing sugar
- Salted butter

How to make Sugar Syrup...

Sugar syrup will be required in a number of your recipes, particularly the desserts. A basic sugar syrup is 2 parts water to 1 part sugar. So to make 600g sugar syrup melt 200g granulated sugar into 400ml water. Bring to the boil, stir occasionally, remove from the heat and leave to cool. It can be kept chilled in the fridge for future use.

How to make the Iced Feta...

Soften the gelatine leaf as per the instructions on the packet. Usually this would mean placing the leaf in a glass of water for 5 minutes, then removing it and squeezing out excess moisture.

Add the roughly chopped feta cheese to the cold sugar syrup with the pre-soaked gelatine. Liquidise well. If you have an ice cream machine then use that to churn. If not, empty the sorbet mixture into a freezer proof container and freeze. Take it out of the freezer every few hours and give it a whisk. This will help prevent it from separating.

How to make the Tart...

Roll out the puff pastry to a 20cm x 40cm rectangle. Place onto a baking sheet and then place another on top. Weigh it down with a brick. This will give us a lovely flaky pastry that is completely flat, if we leave uncovered it will rise. Bake in the oven at 200°C until golden. Remove from the oven.

Peel and slice the beetroot into discs of approx 1cm. In a shallow dish melt enough butter to completely cover the beetroot discs. Place the beetroot inside and cook at 85°C for about 1 hour until soft.

Finishing up...

When the pastry has cooled, sprinkle it lightly with icing sugar. Place it under a hot grill and allow the pastry to caramelise. Remove from the grill.

Carefully arrange the beetroot on top of the pastry. Place back under the grill until the beetroot is hot. Slice the beetroot tart and place on serving plates. Generously grate the zest of the oranges over the tart. Serve with a scoop of the iced feta cheese.

Lyonnaise Salad

'Salade Lyonnaise' is one of the most popular salads in small French bistros. Originating from Lyon, famed for being France's gastronomical capital, it is typically found on the menus of little eateries called bouchons.

Difficulty level 3

Most recipes you will come across for this use the salad leaf frisee. The original recipe however calls for dandelion leaves. The young golden leaves of the dandelion are used, not the great big ones you will see on the side of the road. In French, the leaves are called 'pissenlit' which literally translates to 'pee in the bed', because it is thought that overconsumption made you wee more.

What you'll need... (Serves 4)

- 50g Dijon mustard
- 25g clear honey
- Large bunch of dandelion leaves or, if not available, 1 head frisee, washed and separated
- 5 rashers thick smoked bacon
- 3 shallots
- 4 slices thick white bread, diced
- Poached hens eggs, 1 per person
- Knob of butter

How to do it...

1. In a frying pan, melt a knob of butter. When it is bubbling add the diced bread and cook until caramelised. Drain on to kitchen paper.

2. Cut the bacon into thin strips and slice the onions finely.

3. Add more butter to the frying pan and cook the bacon and shallots. Remove from the pan and drain on kitchen paper.

4. Mix together the honey and mustard in a large bowl.

5. Add the bacon and onions, Add the dandelion leaves.

6. Mix thoroughly with your hands.

7. Serve into individual bowls, add a poached egg on top and a scattering of the croutons.

CAULIFLOWER COUSCOUS

This is really easy and an interesting use of cauliflower. For a colourful dish try using the purple variety. When you serve this in a large bowl for guests to help themselves too they will undoubtedly ask 'what is it?' That's because it bears such little resemblance to cauliflower as we would normally use it.

Difficulty level 2

WHAT YOU'LL NEED... (SERVES 4)

- Finely grated raw cauliflower
- Handful pomegranate seeds
- Olive oil

- Herb mix of finely chopped chive, tarragon & parsley
- Salt

HOW TO DO IT...

1. Grate the whole cauliflower head using a normal grater. Place in a large bowl and add the seeds from one whole pomegranate.

2. Drizzle with olive oil and stir. Season to taste with sea salt. Serve.

WHY NOT TRY BROCCOLI COUSCOUS?

Again, this is so easy. Using broccoli and different ingredients gives us a different flavour.

WHAT YOU'LL NEED... (SERVES 4)

- Finely grated raw broccoli
- Cup of pistachio nuts shelled
- Olive oil

- Icing sugar
- Herb mix of finely chopped chive, tarragon & parsley
- Salt

HOW TO DO IT...

1. Place the pistachio nuts in a frying pan, sprinkle with icing sugar, heat on medium heat and caramelise. Remove from heat and cool.

2. Add the grated head of raw broccoli to a bowl, throw in the cooled pistachio nuts and herbs. Drizzle with oil and season to taste with the salt. Serve.

LITTLE POTS OF SWEET PEA CREAM & WHITE CHOCOLATE

Difficulty level 3

Not all vegetables need to be cooked in a savoury way. Just think about carrot cake, if you need proof. Hardly anyone notices that it is in fact a cake made from a vegetable. So why not use mushrooms in puddings, asparagus for sweet pies and artichokes for crème brulees?

The reason this is not revolting? All vegetables have natural sugars and carrots have the most. The hardest part to overcome is the association of eating what you would normally have with your Sunday roast, with ice cream or custard. The Black Eyed Peas are a really cool hip hop quartet who have sold over 7.5 million albums worldwide.

WHAT YOU'LL NEED… (SERVES 6)

- 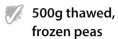 500g thawed, frozen peas
- 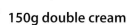 150g double cream
- 140g white chocolate
- 42g sugar
- 2 eggs
-  1 leaf gelatin
- 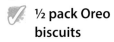 ½ pack Oreo biscuits

HOW TO DO IT…

1. Take a saucepan and place 150g of the peas and 150g double cream. Bring to the boil.
2. Once boiled leave to cool then blend in a food processor. To make the cream smooth, pass through a sieve.
3. Take the remaining 350g peas and boil simply in water for 2 minutes. Drain then whizz in a blender to make a puree. You now have a pea cream and a pea puree.
4. Place the sieved pea cream, the eggs, white chocolate and sugar in a round bottomed pan over hot water and stir with a whisk until the chocolate has melted and it has the texture of thick custard.
5. Soften the gelatine leaf as per the instructions on the packet. Add the pea puree to the pea cream. Drop in the softened gelatin leaf and stir well.
6. Pour mixture into moulds and allow to chill in the refrigerator.
7. Separate the Oreo biscuits into half with cream, halves without. Eat the halves with cream. It's your treat for working hard in the kitchen.
8. In a clean, dry bowl, add the dry halves of the Oreo's and pound with the end of a rolling pin until you have what looks like dry soil. Sprinkle a good layer of the soil on to the top of the chilled pots of pea cream. Serve, with a really good mint chocolate ice cream.

Red Pepper, Raspberry and Chocolate Mousse

Difficulty level 3

What you'll need... (Serves 6)

- ☑ 1 punnet raspberries, crushed
- ☑ 500g very thinly sliced red bell peppers
- ☑ 250g caster sugar
- ☑ Splash of water

- ☑ 100g dark chocolate
- ☑ 100g milk chocolate
- ☑ 75g salted butter
- ☑ 4 eggs
- ☑ 25g caster sugar

How to do it...

1. Place the sliced bell pepper, 250g caster sugar and about 2 tablespoons of water in a saucepan and cook at simmering point for approx 1.5 hours until reaching the consistency of jam. When cooked, cool and then blitz in a blender.

2. Break the chocolate and chop up the butter into small pieces. Place both into a glass mixing bowl and melt over a pan of hot water. Set aside to cool.

3. Separate the eggs into whites and yolks into different bowls.

4. Add the 25g caster sugar to the yolks and whisk until the mixture becomes paler and thick. Slowly stir the egg yolk mixture into the melted chocolate mixture.

5. Using an electric whisk, beat the egg whites until they are thick and make stiff peaks.

6. Using a metal spoon add one spoonful of the egg white and fold into the chocolate mixture. Continue to add the rest of the egg white mixture, spoonful by spoonful, making sure it is well folded in.

7. Take 6 tall glasses, start by placing crushed raspberries at the bottom. Fill half way with Chocolate mousse then add a layer of the red pepper jam, top with raspberries, layer with more chocolate mousse then finish with a dollop of the jam.

PART 2

The Gastronomical! guide to...

Grizzly Gristle, Marvellous Meat & Bonkers Bones

KNIFE TO SEE YOU...

A few pointers you need to take notice of and respect when it comes to knives.

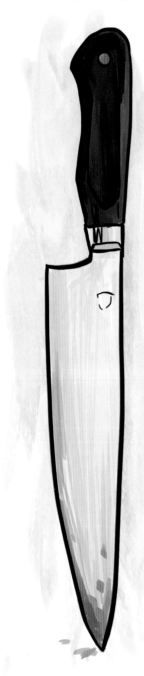

KEEP KNIVES SHARP

If your knife is sharpened properly, it will easily slide through whatever you are cutting, with not too much force. If your knife is blunt, however, you will have to force it and if you slip there is a real danger of cuts.

PUT KNIVES DOWN SAFELY

When working with a knife and you need to put it down, don't put it down with the blade pointing up. Make sure it is away from the surface edge.

<u>NEVER</u> TRY AND CATCH DROPPED KNIVES

If you are handling a knife and you drop it, step back and let it fall, don't try to catch it. The instinct is to try and catch it and that can end up with slices of your hands everywhere.

POINT IT AWAY

When you are using a knife, don't cut towards you or your fingers. Pay attention to where the edge of your sharp blade is pointing and make sure it won't get you if you slip a bit.

DON'T LEAVE SHARP KNIVES LOOSE IN A DRAWER

Clashing around with other kitchen bits and bobs ruins the good sharp edge on your knives. It can also be dangerous if someone who doesn't know they are there reaches into the drawer.

DO NOT PUT KNIVES IN THE SINK

Wash the knives separately. Never leave them in a basinful of soapy water. The unaware person who does the washing up will not thank you when they are dashed to A & E for stitches.

BUYING MEAT

The best way to get fresh meat is to find a reputable butcher. Get to know him or her and purchase from them as often as you can. Most will be happy of the regular custom and will point you in the right direction for the best deal of the day.

STORING MEAT PROPERLY

It is very important to store meat safely to stop bacteria from spreading and to avoid food poisoning, such as salmonella. Here are a few pointers:

- Always wash your hands before and after handling raw meat and fish.

- Store raw meat and poultry in clean, sealed containers on the bottom shelf of the fridge. Doing that prevents the meat from touching other items or dripping raw juices onto other food.

- Follow any storage instructions on the label and don't eat meat after its use by date.

- Always keep cooked meat separate from raw meat.

- Defrost meat thoroughly before cooking. Lots of liquid comes out as meat thaws, so stand it in a bowl to stop bacteria in the juice spreading to other nearby things.

- Never refreeze defrosted meat.

- Use a different chopping board (plastic, not wood) for meats and fish. And always wash it thoroughly, don't simply wipe it.

WHAT'S YOUR BEEF?

Beef is the culinary term given to meat from bovines (otherwise known as cattle). Beef can be harvested from cows (girls), bulls (boys), heifers (young girls) or steers (young boys). Beef cattle are raised purely for meat, not milk production.

Most beef produced in the UK is from crossbred cattle (90%). They grow quickly and, when reared properly, give high quality beef. However, it's not just the prime cuts of meat that we eat. We also eat the liver, heart, kidney, lung, tongue, stomach, pancreas and testicles - I bet you have eaten at least one of these! Many are considered delicacies and in some countries you can ask for a whole calves head to eat – eyes and all!

What do you get if you sit under a cow? A pat on the head!

COW TRIVIA

- ☑ Beef is considered a taboo food in some cultures, especially in Indian culture and is never eaten by Hindus.

- ☑ The United States and Brazil are the top beef producing countries in the world.

- ☑ Cattle outnumber humans in 9 American states: Idaho, Iowa, Kansas, Montana, Nebraska, North Dakota, South Dakota, Oklahoma and Wyoming.

- ☑ The salivary glands of cattle, located beneath the tongue, produce 15 to 20 gallons of saliva per day.

- ☑ The average cow has more than 40,000 jaw movements per day.

- ☑ One cowhide can produce enough leather to make 20 rugby balls, 18 footballs, 18 volleyballs or 12 basketballs.

- ☑ More than 100 modern day medicines, including insulin and oestrogen, are made using cattle by-products.

- ☑ A cow that weighs 1000 pounds will make a carcass weighing about 615 pounds. The carcass makes about 432 pounds of meat.

- ☑ It is not just the obvious food we get from a cow that is important - beef fat, called tallow, is an ingredient in soaps, cosmetics, candles and chewing gum. Bet you thought chewing gum was vegetarian...

- ☑ Cows bones are used to make glue and fertilisers. Blood meal, a fertiliser, is made from blood.

- ☑ Gelatin, made from bones and horns, is used in making sweets, marshmallows, ice cream and photographic film.

MEAT

Some experts believe that if the cow is stressed and tightens its muscles in fear, the meat will not be as good to eat. So they have to be kept as stress free and relaxed as possible.

SLAUGHTER

Killing an animal for food is known as slaughter and we slaughter nearly 7 million cows each year in Britain. That's about a tenth of a cow for every man, woman and child. One steer, a young male cow, can produce enough hamburger meat for 720 quarter-pound hamburgers - enough for a family of 4 to enjoy hamburgers each day for nearly 6 months!

The way we slaughter cows seems truly gruesome but is, in fact, considered to be the least cruel way of killing them. Firstly, they are electrocuted, which makes them unconscious. Then, their throats are cut in order to let all the blood out, this is called 'exsanguination'. The only really grizzly part is that their hearts have to still be pumping for this to work properly. This is why they are knocked out first - their hearts are still pumping but the animal is not aware, nor feels anything.

There are strict laws to make sure that cruelty is not part of the slaughter process. Also, some experts believe that if the cow is stressed, and tightens its muscles in fear, the meat will not be as good to eat. So they have to be kept as stress free and relaxed as possible.

HAMBURGERS

Talking of hamburgers – have you ever wondered why they are called that when there is absolutely no ham in them? The answer is really quite simple – the first hamburgers were made in Hamburg, a city in Germany.

Who actually invented the hamburger remains a mystery. Some say it was a group of nomadic people called the Tartars who tenderised their beef by placing it under a horse's saddle and flattening it into a burger-shaped lump of meat.

Others believe it was the German immigrants who travelled to the United States during the 19th Century, bringing with them their favourite meal called Hamburg Style Beef - a raw chopped piece of beef. Some (bet they are Americans) argue that Americans placed the first cooked beef patty on a roll at the St. Louis World's Fair in 1921.

Whoever invented the hamburger can remain a mystery really because we love them anyway. One company alone, McDonald's, has sold 12 hamburgers for every person in the world and 60% of all sandwiches eaten today are hamburgers.

One small brain, four clever stomachs

Cows are not overly bright, but one area in which they are truly gifted is their stomach. Most people say they have 4 stomachs. The truth is they only have one, but it has four 'compartments' within it.

An adult cow chews grass for 6 hours a day – the mashed food then rests in their first 'stomach' (the Rumen). After a short amount of time the cow 'sicks' this lovely mixture BACK into its mouth and chews it – this is called 'chewing the cud'. A cow will spend 8 hours a day chewing this grass mixture. The Rumen, by the way, is the largest part of the stomach and holds up to 50 gallons of partially digested food. That's a lot of regurgitation – nice!

The second part of the stomach is called the Recticulum – it's also known as the 'hardware' stomach. They need this to protect them from themselves. As we now know cows are not the cleverest of animals and they have a habit of eating stones, bits of fences and stray metal objects. This stomach 'holds' them there. Even though it is not a perfect design, it prevents any further attempts to digest them.

Then we have the Omasum. This part of the stomach is a 'filter'. It filters through all the food the cow eats. The cud is also pressed and broken down further.

Finally, there is the Abomasum - this part of the stomach is like a human's stomach and is connected to the intestines. Here, the food is finally digested by the cows' stomach juices and essential nutrients that the cow needs are passed through to the bloodstream. The rest is passed through to the intestines and produces a 'cow pat'. One cow can produce 4 tons of manure in a year! With the equivalent of four average-sized cars coming out of your bottom a year you'd moo too!

THE REVENGE OF THE COW

Seeing as we have been merrily killing cows to eat, it seems only fair that they get to be part of our downfall. In a cunning plan to rid the earth of us humans, cows are farting and burping their way to our destruction. It's a proven fact that our planet is warming up. Many scientists agree that this is because of greenhouse gases, including methane. Which takes us back to our farting cows. One of the gases found in farts and burps is methane. Whilst a certain amount of methane in the atmosphere is natural and a good thing, when there is too much around, along with other greenhouse gases, it collects in the sky and traps warm air around our planet, which results in global warming. Some scientists believe that cow farts are causing more global warming than pollution from cars. It's a good job they don't drive as well!

VEAL

Veal is the meat of young cattle (calves), as opposed to beef from older cattle. Though veal can be produced from a calf of either sex and any breed, most veal comes from male calves of dairy cattle breeds.

Milk fed veal has a tender texture and a creamy flesh, and comes from cattle slaughtered between 18 and 20 weeks of age. Rose veal is from calves reared on farms in association with the UK RSPCA's Freedom Food programme. Its name comes from its pink colour, which is a result of the calves being slaughtered at around 35 weeks.

The famous Austrian dish, Wiener Schnitzel, comprises veal which is tenderised and then coated with egg and breadcrumbs and fried. The Italians and French have been cooking veal since ancient times.

What did the well mannered sheep say to his friend at the field gate?

After ewe!

DON'T LAMB-AST US...

The meat of a sheep in its first year is 'lamb' and at a very early age it is milk-fed lamb. That of a juvenile sheep older than 1 year is 'hogget', and the meat of an adult sheep is 'mutton'. As sheep get older, their meat changes in flavour and texture, and the older the sheep the longer and more slowly it should be cooked.

While sheep meat only accounts for 6% of the world's meat consumption, it is the main meat in regions of North Africa, the Middle East, India and parts of Europe.

The European Union is the world's largest lamb eater and number one importer of lamb. There are over 60 different breeds of sheep bred in the Britain, more than any other country. But we also import a lot of lamb, 99% of which comes from Australia and New Zealand.

People started raising sheep over ten thousand years ago in Central Asia and today there are about 1 billion sheep on the planet. Sheep production is man's oldest organised industry. Wool was the first valuable commodity to warrant international trade - spinning wool into thread began about 5,000 years ago.

So important was the trade that during the 16th and 17th Centuries, England tried to stop the wool industry in the American colonies. However, the American settlers took no notice of that and by 1664 they had 10,000 sheep! The General Court of Massachusetts then passed a law forcing young people to learn to spin and weave and by 1698, America was exporting wool goods. England was enraged and outlawed wool trading. The punishment for continuing to trade involved cutting off a person's right hand (bit harsh!). The restrictions on sheep-raising and wool manufacturing, along with the Stamp Act, led to the American Revolution.

DOLLY THE SHEEP

The most famous sheep in the world was called Dolly. She was the first ever successfully cloned mammal. Normally, mammals reproduce through a process that always involves two parent animals, one male, the other female. Cloning is the production of a new, genetically identical individual from a single parent animal. Dolly was born at the Roslin Institute in Scotland in July 1996. She had three mothers! Yes three. Her genetic mother provided the DNA. A second ewe provided the egg into which the DNA was injected and a third ewe carried the cloned embryo. It took 276 attempts before the experiment was successful and her birth was hailed as a huge scientific breakthrough. She was named Dolly after the famous Country and Western singer, Dolly Parton.

Dolly gave birth to six lambs but was put to sleep when she was six and a half years old after she developed a lung infection. Dolly was stuffed and is now on display in the Royal Museum of Scotland.

OTHER SHEEP FACTS EWE NEED TO KNOW!

- One pound of wool can make ten miles of yarn and there are 150 yards (450 feet) of wool yarn in a baseball.

- The small intestines from 11 sheep are needed to make 1 tennis racket.

- Sheep are born with milk teeth and will grow 2 permanent teeth a year to replace these, until they have 8. At this stage the sheep is said to have a 'full mouth'. When a ewe has lost some of her teeth she is called a 'broken mouth' ewe. When she's lost all her teeth, she's called a 'gummer'.

- Lamb is the lowest in cholesterol of all red meats.

- Raw wool contains 10 to 25 percent grease or 'lanolin', which is recovered during the scouring process. Lanolin consists of a highly complex mixture of esters, alcohol and fatty acids and is used in adhesive tape, printing inks, motor oils and auto lubrication. Lanolin is also used in cosmetics and pharmaceuticals. Many cosmetics and beauty aids, such as lipsticks, mascara, lotions, shampoos and hair conditioners contain lanolin.

- Sheep skins are removed from the carcasses after slaughter. They are treated in a process called tanning and made into soft leather. Sheep skin is commonly used for making the chamois cloth that you wash your car with. A small number of skins are preserved and sold with the wool still attached.

- Sheep cheese accounts for just over 1% of the world's cheese production. Some of the world's most famous cheeses were originally made from sheep's milk including roquefort, feta, ricotta and pecorina romano. Sheep's milk is also made into yogurt, butter and ice cream.

Lucky was the world's oldest sheep. She died in November 2009 at the age of 23, twice the life expectancy of a sheep.

MEAT

NO PORKIES HERE

Around 10,000 years ago wild pigs were tamed and caged for our personal use. They were the first animals ever to be used domestically and at any time, there are probably about 850 million pigs in the world!

We slaughter 14 million pigs a year in Britain. That's nearly a quarter of a pig each for every man, woman and child. That's a lot of sausages and ham sandwiches!

We eat almost every bit of the pig - its flesh, organs, skin and even its' trotters.

There are some religions that will not eat pork or use pig products. Jews, Muslims and even some Christians think that pig flesh is unclean. There are many deeply believed and heart-felt reasons for this but as far as the actual pig is concerned, it is one of the cleanest and most intelligent animals around.

Pigs have been placed fourth on the intelligence list (humans are first, primates are second, dolphins and whales are third and pigs are fourth). Some pigs are known to learn tricks faster and better than dogs.

The reason we see pigs covered in mud is because they have no sweat glands so cannot sweat to cool off (unlike us) and so roll around in muck to cool their skin.

Pigs are also some of the cleanest animals around, refusing to poo anywhere near their living or eating areas when given a choice.

'Big Bill' was an absolute whopper, weighing in at just over a staggering 1,157kg!

PIG TRIVIA

✓ There are pigs on every continent except for Antarctica.

✓ The largest pig was a hog named Big Bill. He weighed a portly 2,552 lbs and was so large that he dragged his belly on the ground. He had a shoulder height of over 1.5 metres and a length of over 2.7 metres.

✓ A mother pig can give birth to 8 - 12 piglets in one litter and she may have 2 litters in every year. On one occasion, one mother pig gave birth to 37 piglets at the same time.

✓ Pigs have four toes on each trotter but only walk on two of their toes. They look like they are walking on tiptoe.

✓ A domesticated pig has approximately 15,000 taste buds, which is more than any other mammal, including humans.

✓ Piglet from Disney's Winnie-the-Pooh, is the only pig that has ever been known to look up because they lack the ability to do so.

✓ Wild pigs will eat bulbs, roots, fungi, eggs, birds, rodents, fruit, snails, carrion and snakes.

✓ Pork refers to any meat that comes from a pig. Fresh cuts (like pork chops) and processed cuts (like ham and bacon) come from different sections of the pig, but they are all considered pork.

A PIGS HEART IS BETTER THAN NONE

A pig's heart is located in the pig's chest cavity. If a pig were to stand up tall on its hind two legs, its heart would be in the same place that your heart is when you stand up. The interesting thing is that a pig's heart is very similar to a human's heart. So similar in fact that there are humans walking around today with pig heart valves in their bodies, which replaced their own damaged or diseased valves.

Pig's livers (which we also eat) have been used to support human livers in very sick people. They filter blood in exactly the same way and are biologically very similar. People with insulin-dependent diabetes usually inject themselves with pig insulin. Insulin is a hormone produced by the pancreas that regulates the level of glucose, a simple sugar that provides energy, in the blood.

Pigs are so biologically similar to us that medical students and scientists study pig organs and use their hearts, livers and eyes to represent the human versions in experiments.

TOO CHICKEN?

There are more chickens in the world than there are of any other domesticated bird. In fact, there's more than one chicken for every human on the face of this earth. China is the most populated country in the world, so also has the most chickens. There are over 3,000,000,000 chickens in China! Americans eat 8 billion chickens a year.

Chickens can live quite a long time – about the same as a dog or cat, that's about 10 to 15 years, though it can be 20.

The male, known as a cockerel, is larger and more brightly-coloured than the female, which is known as a hen. This is a common feature in birds, as the males use their colourful plumage to attract the females. It is often felt that nature has been really unfair to the female birds; making them really dull, plain and, well, frankly a bit ugly! Of course this doesn't happen in the human world where girls really are much prettier than boys!

Hens don't need a male to be productive either, they can lay eggs without a cockerel being around. He only comes in handy if chicks are needed. Once the egg is laid, the hen turns it about 50 times in a day. Have you ever wondered why the yolk is always in the middle of the egg? Turning the egg makes sure the yolk doesn't stick to the shell.

Not just chickens

Poultry is the term used to describe domesticated birds kept by humans for the purpose of collecting their eggs or killing for their meat. These most typical are chickens, quails, turkey, domestic ducks and domestic geese. Poultry can also include other birds which are killed for their meat, such as pigeons, or birds considered to be game, like pheasants and partridge.

The word Poultry comes from the French word 'poule', which means small animal.

Wild Meats and Game

Not all of the meat we eat is from farmed or domesticated animals. Some is caught or shot out in the wild. These meats can be a bit tougher than their farmed counterparts because, by nature, they move around a lot more and have stronger muscles.

Game and wild meats also tend to be much leaner too. For example hare and rabbit have quite powerful muscles and produce very lean meat.

Deer, of which the meat is commonly known as venison, produces a very rich, flavoursome and lean meat. Interestingly, the word venison can actually mean any wild game. However we tend to use it nowadays to refer to the meat from fallow or roe deer.

Game falls into two types - feathered and furred. There are key dates that must be adhered to that surround game shooting. The season for wild feathered game starts officially on the 12th August - known as the Glorious 12th, and runs through to late February. The season for furred game is between August 1st and late April.

Meat and, in particular, game, is tenderised by being allowed to 'hang' for a period of time so that its flavour develops. The alternative to this is to eat it immediately, before rigor mortis stiffens the animals' muscles. The length of time meat should hang largely depends on how much fat there is. More than a few days will spoil a piece of meat if it is lean like veal or lamb. However, beef and mutton are sometimes 'aged' for many weeks.

During hanging, the meat begins the process of breaking down. What this means is that the meat is more tender, but if it is left for any extra time can develop a pungent flavour. This flavour is particularly enjoyable in birds, such as pheasant. After your wild meat has been hung for your chosen amount of time, there is just one more thing to look out for - tiny pieces of shot. These creatures are killed by shooting and sometimes a small piece of shot can be bedded down in the meat, it is not harmful, just a shock to come across and many a tooth has been broken chomping down on a piece of lead.

MEAT

TRIVIA

✔️ A great way to show off your knowledge of chickens and eggs is to tell someone which hen will lay a brown egg and which a white one! The prediction is not as difficult as it sounds actually – just look at their earlobes. Their ears aren't visible but the lobes can be seen on the side of the head! A chicken with red earlobes will lay brown eggs, and a chicken with white earlobes will produce white eggs.

✔️ Most chickens will stop laying eggs when the weather is cold. They will start laying again when it gets warmer. A hen lays an average of 300 eggs per year.

✔️ If an egg is fertilised, it will start developing into a chicken when its temperature reaches 86 degrees Fahrenheit. A chick takes 21 days to hatch.

✔️ Although the male chicken is more beautiful, it is considered to be less useful. If there is more than one cockerel in a pen, they fight each other and are very aggressive – sometimes attacking humans. The only answer is to get rid of the male you don't want.

✔️ Cockerels often have to be kept separate from the hens as they can attack them too but they are good to have around. Hens feel safer and happier if there is a male hanging about. When there isn't a cockerel, one of the female chickens will take on the male role. She will stop producing eggs and even start to crow – though the crow will be a bit girly!

✔️ Cooked cockscombs are a delicacy in France.

✔️ In Gainesville, Georgia - the chicken capital of the world - it is illegal to eat chicken with a fork.

✔️ According to National Geographic, scientists have settled the old dispute over which came first - the chicken or the egg. They say that reptiles were laying eggs thousands of years before chickens appeared, and the first chicken came from an egg laid by a bird that was not quite a chicken. That seems to answer the question. The egg came first.

✔️ The closest living relative of the T-Rex is the chicken.

✔️ The chicken pox wasn't named after chickens and doesn't have anything to do with chickens. The name came from an old English expression 'gican pox', meaning 'itching pox'.

Mike the Headless Chicken

In Fruita, Colorado, the town folk celebrate 'Mike the Headless Chicken Day'. Seems that in 1945 when a farmer cut off Mike's head in anticipation of a chicken dinner, Mike lived for another 4 years!

It's not awful, it's Offal

Cows, chickens, pigs and lambs are not just made up of the finest cuts of meat. They are not just fillets and breasts. There are many parts of these animals that would make you want to run a mile screaming 'YUCK'. These bits are commonly known as offal. No not awful, offal!

Livers are probably the best known of this group. They are often made into pâtés or mousses. Kidneys too are quite commonly used in pies but we try to never really think about where they have come from, or what they were once used for in the living creature! Marrowbone can be eaten, as can tongues, ears, hearts, stomachs, testicles, glands and brains! They may not be the nicest looking parts of an animal but they are tasty and delicious.

Heart

As we know the heart is a very hard-working muscle, but because of that, it can be quite tough and rubbery. As with all pieces of meat that get a good workout, it is best cooked slowly, being stewed or braised. The longer it cooks the more tender it becomes. Again it is full of goodness. Heart is low in sodium and very high in iron. It also contains selenium, zinc, phosphorus, niacin and riboflavin.

Tripe

This is a variety of stomach and intestinal tissue. It is eaten with gusto in almost every country in the world. It can be deep fried, boiled, roasted, curried – you name it, you can do it with tripe. It used to be eaten by poorer people in Britain because it is a cheap form of protein. For many years it has been ignored by most of us, though it appears to be making a comeback in many posh restaurants. Tripe must be washed properly – boiling it in water with some salt will clean it and soften it beautifully. Your butcher is the best person to get it from. It contains vitamin B12 and significant amounts of protein. You have almost certainly eaten tripe – whether you know it or not.

BRAINS

Hard working or not, brains are a real delicacy in many parts of the world, especially Asia and Europe. The French love calves' brains, particularly in provincial cooking. We have strict rules in Britain about which brains we can and cannot eat, however if you get them from a reputable source they can be delicious and good for you. They are high in niacin, phosphorus and vitamins B12 and C. If you think eating calves' brains is somewhat gruesome, it is actually true (and not just the fantasy of the makers of Indiana Jones) that some people in Africa and Indonesia eat monkey brains!

KIDNEY

Ah, a lovely steak and kidney pie or pudding – you can't beat it on a cold winter's day. The function of a kidney is to help with the extraction of waste products – in simple terms, it makes wee. When cooking kidneys, you can do one of two things. Either fry them quickly or stew them slowly. Anywhere in between, they can become tough. Depending on the animal they came from, they can have a very strong flavour so it is best to disperse them a bit. Stewing them allows them to take on other juices. Preparing a kidney for cooking is fairly simple but you must cut away all connective stringy tissue – once cooked it can turn into a rubber so hard you could make a tyre out of it. Again, your butcher can do this for you. Kidneys are good at providing vitamins B5 and B12.

LIVER

You are more likely to have eaten liver than any other piece of offal. Have you ever had liver and onions? Or pâté? If you have been on holiday to France you may even have eaten foie gras, which is goose liver. Liver can be delicious and it is very, very good for you. It is a great source of iron and vitamins, including vitamin A, which promotes healthy skin, teeth, and eyes. It also contains zinc, vitamin B, vitamin C and vitamin D. Beef liver contains huge amounts of copper and good amounts of healthy fatty acids.

MARROWBONE

Whenever you hear of marrowbone, you probably think about dog food. We are constantly told how good this stuff is for the pooches – but it is delicious and brilliant for us too. It is the flexible tissue found inside bones which produces new blood cells.

Many cultures love bone marrow as a food. In Iranian cuisine, lamb shanks are usually broken before cooking to allow diners to suck out and eat the marrow. In Hungary, tibia (a cow's thigh bone) is a main ingredient of beef soup; the bone is chopped into short pieces and the ends are covered with salt, which keeps the marrow inside the bone while cooking. Upon serving the soup, the marrow is usually dug out and spread on toast.

Some anthropologists believe that early humans were scavengers rather than hunters. Marrow would have been a brilliant food source for early men, who were able to crack open bones using their basic tools.

By the 18th century diners used a marrow scoop, or marrow spoon, often made of silver and with a long thin bowl. That was used as a table implement for removing marrow from a bone. Today, bone marrow is incredibly trendy and is being used in many gourmet kitchens.

SWEETBREADS

Many a dinner party has included an argument about what sweetbreads are. They are glands – one is found in the neck, the other in the pancreas. The neck ones, the proper name is Thymus Glands, are more irregular in shape than pancreas sweetbreads and do not have as much flavour. This is why they cost less than their pancreatic counterparts. Whether from the neck or pancreas, they're taken from pigs, lambs and calves under one year old. Other glands are often called sweetbreads, including cheek glands, tongue glands and testicles. They are considered a gastronomic delight and are served at the finest restaurants. Sweetbreads can be prepared in a number of ways, from sautéing to deep frying.

Tails, Tongues and Trotters

There is no need to ask where these items come from or what they are used for. The tail of an ox is considered, by some, to be the most flavoursome cut of beef. It's also cheap and cheerful – though it won't be wagging in agreement! It is most often sold cut into individual sections following the caudal vertebra, ranging in size from tennis-ball-sized pieces where the tail joins the body (the thick end) to the thumb-sized tip of the tail. Oxtail soup is delicious but this off-cut can be used to create many delicious dishes, such as oxtail ragout, oxtail stews and casseroles.

Have you ever had a tongue sandwich? You may have eaten tongue as a pressed meat (a bit like sliced ham) but many people don't even think about the fact it really came from the tongue of a cow or pig. Tongue is very easy to work with and can be cooked several ways, including smoking, boiling and pickling. We know already that hard working muscles can lead to quite tough meat and the tongue does work hard (think of your own), so slow cooking is the key to making this tough piece of meat lovely and tender. It's cheap to buy and good for you too, boasting loads of iron, some calcium and vitamin C.

Trotters are a delicacy. They are pigs feet, both front and back. They too can be cooked in many ways and are very simple to work with. You can boil them until soft, though do that in a liquid with lots of added flavours. Or you can cover the boiled trotters in butter and bread-crumbs and bake them in the oven. Most delicious though is deep frying or broiling them until the skin is crispy!

MEAT

MEAT RECIPES

IN THIS SECTION...

RECIPES FROM SHAUN HILL

HOW TRICKY ARE THE RECIPES? LOOK OUT FOR THESE...

Difficulty level 1

Difficulty level 2

Difficulty level 3

STOCK PILE

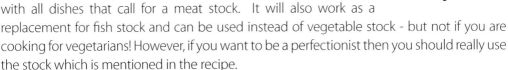

Difficulty level I

Many dishes will call for a stock.

Chicken stock is a great universal stock and will work pretty much with all dishes that call for a meat stock. It will also work as a replacement for fish stock and can be used instead of vegetable stock - but not if you are cooking for vegetarians! However, if you want to be a perfectionist then you should really use the stock which is mentioned in the recipe.

Lamb, beef, and chicken bones are most commonly used for stock. The stock's flavour is derived from the tissues in the bones, which contains collagen. The collagen turns into gelatin during the cooking process, which helps to thicken the stock.

With all meat stocks, you'll need to skim them from time to time. What do we mean? Well, fat rises to the surface of the stock when it is cooking, you will recognise it as a grey murky looking froth. Simply take a ladle and skim the top off the stock and throw it away.

Stocks really do add a great depth of flavour to dishes. It is quite laborious to make good stock but it is worth it. To save a bit of time, when you have made some stock, try freezing it in small quantities.

All stocks adhere to the same method. Firstly, gently caramelise the bones in a very large saucepan, then cover with cold water to about a centimetre above the bones. Add the rest of the ingredients. If using herbs, it's easier and better to tie them together with string, which makes it easier to get them out. Bring to the boil and then simmer for 3 hours, skimming frequently. Drain through a metal sieve.

What you need for Chicken stock...

- ☑ 1 whole chicken carcass
- ☑ 1 carrot chopped roughly
- ☑ 2 onions peeled and in quarters
- ☑ 1 celery stalk chopped roughly
- ☑ Handful fresh flat leaf parsley.

For Lamb / Beef / Veal stock...

- ☑ 900g meat bones
- ☑ 2 onions, roughly chopped
- ☑ 2 carrots, roughly chopped
- ☑ 2 sprigs of fresh thyme
- ☑ 2 sprigs of fresh parsley
- ☑ 6 peppercorns
- ☑ 2 celery sticks, roughly chopped.

BREADED CHICKEN ESCALOPES

Difficulty level 1

WHAT YOU'LL NEED...

- ✓ **4 boneless chicken breasts, skin removed**
- ✓ **10 fresh sage leaves, finely chopped**
- ✓ **12 black peppercorns, crushed**
- ✓ **8 tablespoons plain flour**

- ✓ **2 free-range eggs, beaten**
- ✓ **150ml milk**
- ✓ **250g fresh breadcrumbs**
- ✓ **180g unsalted butter**

MEAT

HOW TO DO IT...

1. Sandwich each chicken breast between two sheets of cling film.

2. Using a rolling pin, flatten each chicken breast until it has widened and become thinner, which is called an escalope. Remove and throw away the cling film.

3. Season the chicken escalopes with the chopped sage and black pepper.

4. Tip the flour into a bowl.

5. Beat the eggs and milk together in a separate bowl.

6. Sprinkle the breadcrumbs onto a plate. These can be made by blitzing bread (ideally stale - or toasted) in a food processor.

7. Dredge each chicken escalope in the flour and shake off any excess.

8. Dip each floured escalope in the egg and milk mixture and then put straight into the breadcrumbs until completely coated.

9. Heat the butter in a frying pan over a medium to high heat. Add the escalopes and fry for approximately 5 minutes on each side. You may need to do this in batches.

10. When the breadcrumbs are crisp and the juices run clear from the chicken it is cooked.

11. Remove from the pan onto kitchen paper to remove excess grease.

12. Squeeze a little fresh lemon juice over and serve with rocket leaves drizzled with olive oil and a few thin slices of parmesan.

ROAST CHICKEN

Many people get this wrong, so here is a great and easy recipe for perfect roast chicken. Before you place the bird inside the oven please make sure there isn't a little pack of innards inside. If there is, then please remove them.

Difficulty level 1

WHAT YOU'LL NEED... (SERVES 6)

✓ **1 medium sized chicken**

✓ **One lemon**

✓ **Salt, 2 teaspoons black pepper**

✓ **Oil (to grease roasting pan)**

✓ **Fresh herbs, your choice - rosemary, thyme, or tarragon**

HOW TO DO IT...

1. Preheat the oven to 200°C and work out your cooking time. You should allow 25 minutes cooking per 450g of weight.

2. Cut away any string or plastic binding your chicken together. Spread the legs out and then place the chicken in a shallow, lightly oiled roasting pan.

3. Sprinkle a little salt and freshly ground pepper inside the cavity of the bird.

4. Slice up one lemon in half and place it inside the cavity.

5. Close the opening with toothpicks.

6. Rub a little salt and pepper onto all sides of the chicken and then turn it upside down back in the roasting tin. Place it in the top third of your oven.

7. After 50 minutes, remove the chicken from the oven, flip it over, and return it to the oven to finish roasting breast-side up.

8. After another 45-50 minutes of cooking, remove the chicken – but double check it is cooked through first. Stick a metal skewer into the thickest part of the chicken – just around the underside of the legs. The juices should always run clear. If there is any pink in them at all put it back in the oven until the juices are perfectly clear.

9. Take the bird out of the pan and leave to 'rest' for at least 20 minutes. Resting allows the meat to pull in all its juices making it soft and tender. It will also carve much more easily without shredding. Use the pan juices for making a lovely gravy by returning to the heat on the stovetop, adding butter and water then stirring all the caramelised chicken juices from the bottom of the roasting pan into it until the right consistency for your gravy.

A family favourite - just don't argue over who gets a leg!

Stack it high
and open wide!

BEEFBURGERS

When making your own beefburgers the most crucial part is buying good meat. Often ready-minced beef contains an awful lot of water and that also applies to pork, lamb and chicken. This is added to make the meat heavier and as we pay by weight, the greedier supermarkets make more money.

Difficulty level 1

Ask your local butcher for a piece of topside or top rump, and don't be alarmed if the meat has a little fat on it. That will add depth of flavour and keep the meat moist whilst cooking. Your butcher will mince the meat for you while you wait.

WHAT YOU'LL NEED… (SERVES 4)

- ☑ **About 600g minced topside of beef**
- ☑ **Two tablespoons of chopped white onion**
- ☑ **Cracked black pepper and sea salt**
- ☑ **30g finely chopped tarragon**
- ☑ **30g finely chopped curly parsley***
- ☑ **Vegetable oil for frying**

HOW TO DO IT…

1. Take the meat out of the fridge and leave it in a covered bowl until it reaches room temperature.

2. Place the chopped onion into a bowl and add both the parsley and the tarragon. The parsley will add a lovely fragrant earthiness to the meat whilst the tarragon will bring a freshness that cuts through the fat. Add a good pinch of salt and a twist or two of black pepper.

3. Mix the mince into the onion and herbs. Don't use a spoon. Use your hands

4. Separate the mixture into 4 even balls and then flatten out the balls into burgers. Make sure the meat is nice, compact and evenly flat.

5. Heat a little oil in the frying pan. Place the burgers in but mind you don't have the oil too hot otherwise they could be cremated on the outside but raw in the middle. Turn the burgers every couple of minutes. They should be done in about 8 minutes but this depends on how well done you want them to be.

6. Serve how you like. We prefer them in baps with some ketchup, sliced gherkin and a cheese slice.

There are two types of parsley, one is called flat leaf and the other curly. The flat leaf has a much stronger flavour than the curly one and as we are using two herbs that we want to complement each other, they should have equal amounts of flavour)

MEAT

Chinese Spiced Pork with Pineapple

Difficulty level 1

What you'll need... (Serves 4)

- 2 teaspoons vegetable oil
- 4 pork steaks
- 2 tablespoons light brown sugar
- 1 teaspoon tomato purée
- 1 can pineapple rings in juice
- ½ teaspoon chilli powder
- 1 teaspoon Chinese five-spice powder
- Coriander leaves, to serve
- 1 tablespoon dark soy sauce

How to do it...

1. Add a drizzle of oil to a flat plate and season with salt and pepper.

2. Add the pork steaks to the oil, cover well on both sides.

3. Heat a frying pan and, when hot, add the pork and fry for 5 minutes on each side until golden.

4. Mix the sugar, soy, tomato purée and juice from the can of pineapples in a bowl. Keep to one side.

5. Add the pineapple rings to the pan and let them caramelise alongside the pork.

6. Add the chilli and five-spice to the pan, then fry for a further minute.

7. Now pour in the soy mix and let it simmer around the pork and pineapple until slightly reduced and sticky.

8. Sprinkle with coriander and serve with steamed or boiled rice.

Beef Bourguignon

Beef bourguignon is one of many examples of peasant dishes being slowly refined into modern restaurant fare. Originating from Burgundy in France, it's a much loved traditional French recipe that's basically a stew prepared with beef braised in red wine (traditionally red Burgundy) and beef broth. It is generally flavoured with garlic and onions.

Difficulty level 2

Cooked slowly, the beef should fall apart. Yum yum in my tum.

WHAT YOU'LL NEED... (SERVES 4)

- ✅ **900g braising steak – cut into 2 inch cubes**
- ✅ **3 tablespoons olive oil**
- ✅ **1 sliced medium onion**
- ✅ **15g plain flour**
- ✅ **425ml red wine**
- ✅ **2 chopped cloves garlic**
- ✅ **1 bay leaf**
- ✅ **2 sprigs thyme**
- ✅ **350g shallots**
- ✅ **225g thick cut streaky bacon (lardons) cut into cubes**
- ✅ **110g large mushrooms**
- ✅ **Salt and pepper**
- ✅ **Pre-heat the oven to 140°C.**

MEAT

HOW TO DO IT...

1. Bring 1¼ tablespoons of the oil to sizzling point in the casserole or pan and brown the beef, a few pieces at a time. Transfer the meat to a plate as it browns – leaving the juices behind in the pan.

2. Once the meat is done add the sliced onion and brown that a little too.

3. Return the meat to the pan and sprinkle in the flour, stirring round to mop up all the juices. Then slowly pour in the wine - stirring all the time – to avoid lumps.

4. Add the chopped garlic, herbs and seasoning, put the lid on and cook very gently on top of the stove or transfer to the oven for two hours.

5. After two hours, add browned bacon and shallots and the raw sliced mushrooms. Cook for a further hour.

6. It is great served with new potatoes and green beans.

MOROCCAN STYLE LAMB

This is a delicious and warming dish full of flavour, very similar to a Tagine recipe. Often dishes that are slow cooked, such as this one, taste even better the next day. So make it then try refrigerating it and reheating the following evening.

Difficulty level 2

If you can wait that long...

WHAT YOU'LL NEED... (SERVES 4)

- ☑ 2 tablespoons olive oil
- ☑ 700ml lamb or chicken stock
- ☑ 550g diced lean lamb
- ☑ 1 chopped onion
- ☑ 2 crushed garlic cloves
- ☑ 1 cinnamon stick

- ☑ 1 teaspoon runny honey
- ☑ 175g dried apricots, chopped
- ☑ Chopped fresh mint – a good handful
- ☑ 25g ground almonds
- ☑ 1 orange

HOW TO DO IT...

1. In a large ovenproof casserole heat the olive oil. Add the diced lamb and brown over a medium-high heat for approximately 5 minutes. Stir the lamb frequently to ensure you get an even covering of colour on the meat.

2. Remove the lamb from the casserole dish and place on a plate – keep to one side.

3. Put the onion and garlic in the unwashed casserole and cook until softened. Add the lamb back. Then add the stock, the cinnamon, the honey and both the juice and zest of 1 orange.

4. Season, bring to the boil then reduce the heat and simmer for approximately 1 hour.

5. Add the apricots. Cook for a further half hour until the meat is so tender it almost falls apart. Stir in the ground almonds, this will make the sauce thicker.

6. Just before serving, stir in the freshly chopped mint.

If you're making this a day prior make sure you don't add the mint - always just put the mint in just before serving.

Lemon Chicken with Homemade Salad Cream

Difficulty level 2

What You'll Need for the Chicken... (Serves 2)

- ✓ 200ml olive oil
- ✓ 2 small red chillies, chopped with their seeds
- ✓ 2 sprigs rosemary, coarsely chopped
- ✓ 4 chicken thighs
- ✓ 1 lemon, zest and juice

How to Do It...

1. Mix the olive oil, lemon zest and juice, chilli and rosemary in a large bowl.

2. Add the chicken thighs to the bowl with the marinade and leave for 2-3 hours.

3. Preheat the oven to 200℃, put the marinated chicken, skin side up, onto a roasting tray and roast for approximately 30 minutes or until clear juices flow from the inside when skewered.

4. Remove from the oven and leave to rest before serving.

What You'll Need for the Salad Cream...

- ✓ 2 eggs
- ✓ 1 tablespoon English mustard powder
- ✓ 1 tablespoon plain flour
- ✓ ½ teaspoon caster sugar
- ✓ 125ml white wine vinegar
- ✓ 50ml vegetable oil
- ✓ 100ml double cream

How to Do It...

1. In a bowl over a pot of boiling hot water, whisk the eggs, mustard and flour for a few seconds until it comes together.

2. Then very slowly add the vinegar and oil. Stir until thick then remove from the heat.

3. Add the sugar. When cool, stir in the double cream. Remove from the oven and leave to rest before serving.

To Assemble...

Place chicken thighs on a plate with a bowl of the salad cream in the centre. Dip the thighs into the salad cream and serve.

BBQ Ribs

Difficulty level 2

Pork ribs are a very popular cut of pork. The ribcage of a domestic pig, meat and bones together, is cut into usable pieces, and then prepared by smoking, grilling, or roasting. The ribs are usually served with a sauce, often barbecue sauce.

Baby back ribs are from the top of the rib cage between the spine and the spare ribs. Spare ribs are taken from the belly side of the rib cage, below the section of back ribs and above the breast bone.

Spare ribs usually have more fat than baby back ribs and are flatter with more bone. Baby back ribs are usually meatier, they come from younger animals 'hogs' rather than 'sows'.

What you'll need... (Serves 2)

- 1 to 1.5kg pork ribs
- 1 tablespoon chopped garlic
- 1 teaspoon ground black pepper
- 2 tablespoons salt
- 250ml of bought BBQ sauce

How to do it...

1. Place ribs in a large pot with enough water to cover. Season with salt.

2. Bring water to the boil and cook ribs until tender.

3. Remove ribs from pot, and place them in a baking dish with the fresh garlic and a twist of black pepper.

4. Pour BBQ sauce over ribs.

5. Cover dish with aluminium foil and bake in the preheated oven for approximately 1 ½ hours at 180°C.

If you like these, why not try the sticky ribs on the next page?

MEAT

Some food is best eaten with your hands - this is definitely one of them!

Sticky Ribs
– A Bit Trickier...

Difficulty level 2

If you fancy having a go at making the whole recipe, including the sticky BBQ sauce then try this one.

What You'll Need... (Serves 4)

- **2kg pork loin rib racks, cut into blocks of 4**
- **100g soft brown sugar**
- **100ml dry sherry**
- **100g fresh ginger, peeled and finely grated**
- **3 garlic cloves, peeled and crushed**
- **200ml tomato ketchup**
- **1 tablespoon Dijon mustard**
- **150ml soy sauce**

How To Do It...

1. Again, put the ribs in a large saucepan with 50ml of soy sauce and cover with cold water. Simmer for 15 minutes, remove from the heat and leave to cool but not go cold.

2. To make the marinade put the sugar and sherry in a small pan and heat gently until the sugar has melted. Add the ginger and the garlic and cook gently for 15 minutes.

3. Add the rest of the cloves, ginger, mustard ketchup and remaining 100ml soy sauce.

4. Stir well and remove from heat after 10 minutes of cooking.

5. Whilst still warm, remove the ribs from the pot and brush generously with some, but not all, of the marinade. Keep what's left of the marinade in a bowl in the fridge.

6. Pack the ribs in a large tray or dish and put in the fridge. Leave overnight.

7. Put the ribs into a large roasting tray and pour over some of the marinade. Roast for 40 minutes at 200°C. Add a little water if the marinade does not quite cover the ribs.

8. During the cooking time, remove from the oven and brush generously with the remaining marinade.

Simple Stroganoff

The original recipe of Beef Stroganoff can be a bit tricky because it relies on perfect timing and instant cooking. This one takes the panic out of the cooking and is just as delicious. The meat used is also cheaper to buy – using chuck steak instead of fillet.

Difficulty level 2

What you'll need... (Serves 4)

- 700g lean chuck steak
- 450g large mushrooms
- 75g butter
- 275ml dry white wine
- 2 large onions
- 275 ml soured cream
- Teaspoon freshly grated nutmeg
- Teaspoon paprika
- Salt and pepper

How to do it...

1. Trim the meat and cut into thin strips, about ¼ inch thick and 2 ½ inches long. Better still ask a butcher to do that for you. Cut the onions in half and slice it into half-moon shapes.

2. Melt the butter in a pan, add the onions and soften for about 5 minutes until they are see-through and slightly golden. Remove it from the saucepan (onto a plate) – but leave the juices behind.

3. Turn the heat up and brown the meat by adding a few slices at a time. Once the meat is browned (not cooked through, just cooked on the outside) turn the heat down and throw the onions back in.

4. Add a little salt and pepper before pouring in the wine. Leave it to simmer with the lid on for about an hour and a half, but stir it occasionally. After that add in your sliced mushrooms, which will add a lot of juice. Put the lid back on and continue to simmer for a further 20-30 minutes.

5. Don't just check the clock, simply test the meat for flavour and softness so that you know when it is done. Add more salt and pepper, if you think it needs it, then take it off the heat.

6. Pour in the sour cream and as much nutmeg as you like. Stir the cream though.

7. Serve with plain white rice or mashed potatoes.

Bolognese Sauce

Difficulty level 2

Once you have mastered the art of this traditional pasta sauce, which is originally from Bologna, Italy, then a world of delicious dishes opens up to you. Not only will you be able to make the traditional spaghetti Bolognese but also lasagne, chilli, pizzas and more. You can serve it in jacket potatoes for a lazy cottage pie and we even know of a few people who simply serve it between two slices of thick cut crusty bread.

Our trick to the best bolognese sauce? Add a good dollop of tomato ketchup and a teaspoon of Marmite to it. Just don't tell the Italians..

What you'll need... (Serves 4)

- ☑ **500g minced beef**
- ☑ **1 large onion, 1 large carrot, 2 stalks celery**
- ☑ **500ml tomato passata (sieved tomato)**
- ☑ **2 chopped cloves garlic**
- ☑ **Olive oil**
- ☑ **Knob of butter (1 tablespoon)**
- ☑ **Salt and pepper**
- ☑ **Tablespoon tomato ketchup**
- ☑ **Teaspoon Marmite**
- ☑ **400g can chopped tomatoes**

How to do it...

1. Peel the onion and carrot and wash the celery. Cut into small, even 1cm sized pieces.

2. Heat your flat bottomed frying pan with a little olive oil until it gets hot, but not smoking.

3. Add your meat in and spread it across the surface of the pan. Try not to stir too much, just every 3 minutes or so. The meat will turn from pink to brown.

4. Add your chopped vegetables, put a lid on, turn down and let the meat and vegetables simmer for about another 5 minutes.

5. Pour in the passata, season with salt and pepper. Leave to cook for another 10 minutes. Add the can of chopped tomatoes. Then, when nobody is looking, give a good squirt of ketchup, add the Marmite and stir in.

Steak Tartare

Difficulty level 2

Not all beef needs to be cooked. In fact, beef is probably the only butchers' meat you should ever consider eating raw as there are very real risks of food if you eat undercooked chicken or pork. Lamb can be served pink, as can almost all game meat, but lamb would be quite unpleasant served raw.

The name 'tartare' comes from an ethnic group of people from Asia called 'Tartars' or 'Tatars'. They were very busy people and didn't have much time to cook, so placed the raw meat underneath the horses saddle. The meat would be so tenderized by the end of the ride that cooking was not at all necessary.

In France this dish is made using one of two different kinds of meat - beef or horse. We don't have a market for horse meat yet in Britain so you will probably have to use beef. Campaigners and members of the Royal Family are calling for the use of horsemeat in the UK, however, as bizarrely it would be beneficial for general horse welfare. If horsemeat is considered valuable as a food stuff, people are less likely to neglect them.

What you'll need... (Serves 4)

- 400g finely chopped skirt steak (the piece of meat at the very end of the fillet steak)
- 35g shallots / onions, finely chopped
- 35g finely chopped gherkins
- 50g combined of chopped tarragon, parsley, chive and mint

- 1 tablespoon capers
- 1 Dessertspoon tomato ketchup
- 1 Dessertspoon Dijon mustard
- Olive oil
- Sea salt and black pepper

How to do it...

1. Extremely simple. Put all of the beef, onion, gherkins, capers and herbs together in a bowl. Add about 2 tablespoons of ketchup then add 1 tablespoon of Mustard and a teaspoon of olive oil.

2. Mix all the ingredients together.

To Assemble...

1. Divide the mixture into quarters and mould into perfect circles by packing into large round biscuit cutters in the centre of a plate. Remove the cutter to leave your perfect circle of mixture.

2. For the authentic touch, place a very fresh, raw egg yolk on top of each. Serve with toast.

How long can you resist cutting into the egg yolk?

Roast Loin of Pork with Sweet Onions

Difficulty level 2

What You'll Need... (Serves 4)

- 2kg boned and rolled leg of pork, skin well-scored
- A little olive oil and sea salt
- A handful of thyme sprigs
- 16 shallots, whole but peeled
- 1 head of garlic, halved
- 500ml bottle of cider
- A little cornflour
- Soy sauce, to flavour

How to Do It...

1. Set the oven to 220°C.

2. Rub a little oil, then salt into the skin of the pork, and push thyme sprigs into the meat where you can.

3. Allow cooking time of 25 minutes per 500g, plus 25 minutes. Roast the pork as high up in the oven as it will go for the first hour, then turn the oven down to 190°C for the rest of the cooking time.

4. Add the whole shallots and garlic halves to the meat tin for the last hour of the meat cooking.

5. When cooked, transfer the pork to a warmed plate, and leave in a warm place to rest for at least 15 minutes before carving.

6. Put the shallots and garlic in a warm bowl. Drain off fat from roasting tin, pour juices into a pan, add cider and let it reduce by a third.

7. Add the cornflour a little at a time and stir until thickened. It needs to be the consistency of runny honey, not as thick as a béchamel sauce.

8. Add a dash of soy sauce to flavour.

Sizzling Beef with Broccoli

Difficulty level 2

What you'll need... (Serves 2)

- 500g piece topside beef, thinly sliced across the grain
- 1 tablespoon soy sauce
- 3 teaspoons cornflour
- 1 teaspoon sesame oil
- 1 teaspoon cracked black pepper
- 2 tablespoons peanut oil
- 1 onion, halved, cut into thin wedges
- 4 garlic cloves, crushed
- 1 handful coarsely chopped fresh chives
- 1 bunch broccoli cut into 4cm lengths
- 160ml vegetable stock
- 2 tablespoons sweet soy sauce
- Steamed rice, to serve

How to do it...

1. Combine the beef, soy sauce, cornflour, sesame oil and pepper in a large bowl. Marinade for 30 minutes in the fridge.

2. Heat 3 teaspoons of the peanut oil in a wok over high heat until just smoking. Add half the beef mixture and stir-fry for 1-2 minutes or until brown. Transfer to a heatproof bowl. Repeat with 3 teaspoons of the remaining oil and the remaining beef mixture, reheating wok between batches.

3. Heat the remaining oil in the wok over a medium-high heat until just smoking. Add the onion and stir-fry for 2 minutes or until soft.

4. Add the garlic and half the chives and stir-fry for 1 minute or until aromatic. Add broccoli and stock and stir-fry for 3 minutes or until broccoli is bright green and tender crisp.

5. Return beef to the wok along with the sweet soy sauce and remaining chives and stir-fry for 1 minute or until mixture boils and thickens.

6. Serve immediately with steamed rice.

MEAT

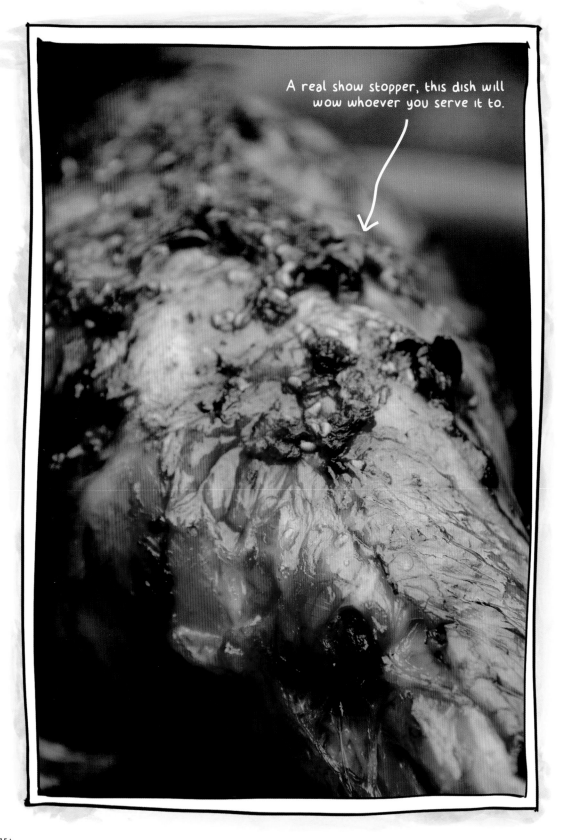

Leg of Lamb with Berries and Honey

Difficulty level 3

What you'll need… (Serves 6)

- ✓ 1 lean whole lamb leg joint approximately 1.3kg in weight
- ✓ 2 fresh rosemary sprigs
- ✓ 2 large garlic cloves, peeled and cut into slivers
- ✓ 6 shallots, peeled and cut into small wedges
- ✓ 30ml or 2 tablespoons olive oil

- ✓ 150ml white wine
- ✓ 900g red potatoes, skin on and cut into wedges
- ✓ 100g fresh blackberries, raspberries or blueberries
- ✓ 30ml or 2 tablespoons runny honey
- ✓ Grated zest and juice of 1 lime

How to do it…

1. Preheat the oven to 200°C.

2. Place the lamb on a chopping board and make several slits all over the joint – stuff them with the rosemary and garlic. Season with salt and pepper.

3. Put the onions in a large non-stick roasting tin and place the joint on top of them.

4. Scatter the potatoes around the joint, throw in the olive oil and white wine.

5. Cover in foil and place in the oven.

6. Cook for 30 minutes.

7. Remove the foil, turn the oven down to 170°C and cook for a further 50 – 60 minutes

8. In a small bowl mix together the berries, honey, lime zest and juice, gently mash with a fork and set aside.

9. Twenty minutes before the end of the cooking time, spread the berry mixture over the lamb and return it to the oven.

10. Remove the joint and vegetables from the oven, transfer to a serving dish, wrap loosely in foil and allow to rest for 20 minutes before carving and serving.

MEAT

Chicken & Mushroom Pie

Difficulty level 3

What you'll need… (Serves 4)

- 1 whole chicken
- 1 onion, halved
- 1 large carrot, peeled
- 1 stick of celery, sliced
- Few sprigs of parsley
- 25g of butter
- 3 tablespoon plain flour

- 250g button mushrooms, halved
- 300g ready-made shortcrust pastry
- Handful fresh chopped flat leaf parsley
- 1 egg, beaten
- Salt and freshly ground black pepper

Best served with mash, green vegetables and lashings of gravy!

How to do it...

1. Place the chicken in a large pot with the onions, carrot, celery and parsley and cover with about 1600ml water.

2. Bring to the boil, then gently simmer it for 1 hour or until the chicken is tender.

3. Remove the chicken from the pan, cool slightly, then use a knife and fork to carefully remove the skin and all the meat from the bones.

4. Throw away the bones and skin.

5. Drain the stock and throw away the vegetables.

6. Place the stock in a pan and fast boil for 25 minutes, or until you see the quantity has reduced by about two thirds. You should have about a pint of stock.

7. Melt the butter in a pan, stir in the flour and let it bubble for a couple minutes. Pour in the stock slowly and bring to the boil, whisking all the time until the sauce thickens.

8. Reduce the heat, stir in the mushrooms and leave to gently simmer for 5 minutes.

9. Cut the chicken into bite sized chunks and stir into the sauce with the parsley.

10. Roll out the pastry on a lightly floured surface.

11. Place an oval pie dish (about 2-3 pint sized one) in the centre of the pastry face down and roughly cut around it. Now, cut strips from the pastry remaining to fit around the rim of the dish. Brush the rim of the pie dish with egg wash (egg beaten with a tablespoon of milk), then stick the pastry strips to it.

12. Spoon the chicken filling into the dish. If you have a ceramic pastry lifter (something that holds the pastry off the filling) place it in the middle of the dish – buried in the filling. Brush the pastry edges with water then lay your big piece of pastry on top.

13. Use a fork to press the two edges of the pastry together to seal. Brush the top of the pie with egg wash. Using a sharp knife cut a small 1 cm hole in the centre of the pie or on both sides of your pastry lifter - this will let the steam out during cooking and stop the pastry from becoming soggy.

14. Place on a baking tray in the oven at 200°C and bake for 25 minutes or until the pastry is golden brown.

15. Serve with steamed green vegetables and some buttery mash.

MEAT

DEVILLED LAMB KIDNEYS ON BUTTERED BRIOCHE

Difficulty level 2

Originally a Victorian breakfast dish, this is a really quick recipe to make and just as tasty as those puffed up rice based breakfast cereals…

WHAT YOU'LL NEED… (SERVES 2)

- **4 lambs kidneys, cleaned and cut into chunks**
- **15ml extra virgin olive oil**
- **5ml mango chutney**
- **5ml curry paste**
- **15ml Worcestershire sauce**
- **15ml hot water**
- **Grated zest of ½ lemon**
- **Salt and freshly milled black pepper**
- **4 slices of thick brioche, lightly toasted and buttered**
- **Fresh tarragon leaves**

HOW TO DO IT…

1. Heat the oil in a large shallow frying pan and cook the kidneys for 3-4 minutes or until brown.

2. Add the chutney and curry pastes, Worcestershire sauce, hot water, lemon zest and seasoning. Heat through for 1-2 minutes.

HOW TO ASSEMBLE…

1. Spoon the mixture over the brioche, scatter with finely chopped tarragon.

2. Serve immediately.

Shaun Hill outside the
Walnut Tree

Part 2 - Grizzly Gristle, Marvellous Meat & Bonkers Bones

Recipes from Shaun Hill

The Walnut Tree Restaurant sits on the B4521, two miles East of Abergavenny: a hustling, bustling market town in Wales. The Walnut Tree has been a famous inn and restaurant since it opened in the early 1960s, when Italian chef Franco Taruschio was at the helm. A proud white building on a sharp corner with a sloping carpark and pretty, ornamental plants, the Walnut Tree gleams in the sunshine.

Born in 1947, Shaun loved cooking for a few reasons. Firstly, he loved good food and was a keen spectator of and contributor to his family's cooked dinners. Secondly, as a teenager cooking offered Shaun a chance to earn some spare cash. Along with his great friend, the late Poet Laureat, Ted Hughes, Shaun would make sandwiches at London Zoo. I am certain that at that time Shaun never anticipated how great his career would be.

Shaun started cooking professionally at Carriers restaurant in 1968, before moving to the famous Gay Hussar, then the Capital Hotel. Leaving London for the Lygon Arms in Broadway, Shaun and his wife Anja opened their own restaurant, Hills, in Stratford-upon-Avon in 1983.

With a young family in tow, Shaun uprooted in 1985 and accepted the position of Head Chef at Gidleigh Park in Chagford, Devon.

Having loved the town of Ludlow for a few years, Shaun and Anja decided to leave Devon in 1994 for Shropshire and opened a tiny cottage restaurant in their new home. The Merchant House operated from a domestic kitchen with only Shaun cooking. The restaurant had only 6 tables. It was fully booked 6 months in advance and was voted 14th best restaurant in the world.

Shaun closed the Merchant House in 2005 and now co-owns and cooks at the Walnut Tree. Previously a consultant to Fortnum & Mason, Shaun is heralded as the 'Godfather' by almost every chef in the industry.

Not bad for a boy who began by making sandwiches at a zoo.

A FEW WORDS FROM
SHAUN HILL

CHEF / PATRON OF THE WALNUT TREE INN, ABERGAVENNY.

Chefs don't joke about food. The idea of food as fun is alien, like comparing golf to a rather long walk or a game of soccer to a pleasant Saturday afternoon's sport. We are too close to the subject to have any objective opinion and a lifetime of obsessing about culinary minutiae qualifies you for the funny farm more than any light hearted banter on food.

But food is a joy. The transformation of raw ingredients to great meals is exciting and universally relevant. Naturally, the sooner small people catch on to this the better.

Meat forms the focal point, usually the main course, of any meal in which it features. It's expensive and calls for the slaughter of a healthy living creature. If this thought spoils your appetite then it shouldn't. It's the way things are and the most thoughtful thing we can do is to treat the ingredient, whether it is a steak or whether it is mince or offal with some respect. Careless cooks in any case are punished by having to eat mediocre meals. Lazy cooks will pay more for someone else to do the work. The best deal is always for those who make an effort.

Avoid all books and recipes that announce they are quick and easy, low calorie or low fat. Well made corned beef hash or spag-bol is a treat and no huge amounts of either time or money are involved. Good food almost invariably has all the healthy and nutritious stuff you need. Even sweet or fatty things are important in moderation.

Chefs in restaurant or hotel kitchens work differently from normal people in their homes. They spend all day in the kitchen making sauces and suchlike, tubs of skinned, de-seeded then diced tomato, chopped shallot, veal and chicken stock reduced gravy jobs like jus or demi glace. Then they can assemble complex dishes and treatments in minutes once an order arrives in the kitchen from the dining room. This is real enough but sometimes impractical for those with lives to lead.

So there you have it. Bin the slimming magazines and only use recipes from chefs whose names begin with Shaun and end with Hill. National treasures such as Delia Smith and Jane Grigson are of course excused.

Shaun Hill

CROMESQUIS

This is a Polish or Russian dish in origin that became popular in France at one time. It also became a handy restaurant device to put leftovers to good use. The idea is to make a small amount of thick white sauce, flavour it with herbs and mustard then add chopped bits of chicken, ham, rabbit, leeks or mushrooms, whatever you have that is both cooked and surplus to requirement. Leave this to cool then when it has set solid to form into patties, breadcrumb and fry. The result will have a softer filling than any fishcake or rissole but with a crisp outer coating. Nice with some salad in sharp dressing.

WHAT YOU'LL NEED... (SERVES 4)

- 250g cooked chicken and ham
- 50g butter
- 30g plain flour
- 100ml milk
- Salt
- Black pepper
- Pinch freshly grated nutmeg
- 1 tablespoon Dijon mustard
- 1 egg – beaten
- 100g fresh breadcrumbs – or panko Japanese crumbs

HOW TO DO IT...

1. Make a roux by melting the butter then stirring in the flour. Let this cook a few moments before adding half the milk.

2. Stir until thick and smooth then add the remaining milk and continue to stir.

3. Dice the leftovers and add along with the mustard and seasonings.

4. Leave to cool and set.

5. Form patties (burger shapes) with the mixture then pass these firstly through beaten egg and then breadcrumbs.

6. Fry until golden and serve with the salads.

Part 2 - Grizzly Gristle, Marvellous Meat & Bonkers Bones

Minced Pork Meatballs
with Haricots, Marjoram and Garlic

Difficulty level 3

Minced anything is a bit of a worry, for there is no doubt that what can
be minced or covered with pastry may not be the finest meat. If possible court a little
unpopularity with the butcher, or the butchery end of the supermarket, by asking for some
shoulder or belly pork then having it minced for you. Fat is good. It makes the meatball
tender and sweet.

What you'll need... (Serves 4)

- 500g minced pork
- 2 cloves garlic – crushed
- 1 teaspoon marjoram or oregano which if more or less the same
- Salt and pepper
- Oil for frying
- 100g smoked streaky bacon – diced
- 50g tinned then drained haricot beans
- 1 chilli – chopped
- 1 teaspoon paprika
- Tin chopped tomatoes
- 25ml water

How to do it...

1. Combine the mince, garlic, marjoram and seasoning.
2. Divide into 12 small patties then fry in oil for 4/5 minutes.
3. Separately, fry the bacon. When it is brown add the paprika and chilli followed by the tomato, water and beans.
4. Place the pork meatballs into this mix and cover with a lid.
5. Cook for 30 minutes then serve.

MEAT

Steak and kidney pudding

Difficulty level 3

One of the world's great dishes. It is not difficult, nor is it particularly quick to make.

What you'll need for the pastry... (Serves 4)

- ✅ 250g self raising flour
- ✅ 1 teaspoon baking powder
- ✅ 115g shredded suet
- ✅ About 100ml iced water

How to do it...

1. Use a food processor to mix the flour and baking powder then add suet and enough water to make a soft dough.

2. Roll out until reasonably thin, keeping back about a quarter of the mix to make the pudding top, which of course will be its base when turned out.

3. Grease an oven proof pudding bowl and then line with the suet pastry. When the filling is ready add this.

4. Moisten the visible edges of the pastry and then cover with the remaining dough. Trim off any excess pastry.

What you'll need for the filling...

- ✅ 1kg diced chuck steak
- ✅ 200g kidney – cleaned , trimmed then diced
- ✅ 1 large onion - chopped
- ✅ 150g button mushrooms
- ✅ 4 tablespoons olive oil
- ✅ 30g plain flour
- ✅ ½ teaspoon each , salt pepper, nutmeg
- ✅ 1 tablespoon Worcestershire sauce
- ✅ 150ml water

How to do it...

1. Fry the onion in olive oil and then brown the meat.

2. Add seasoning and spices, then flour.

3. Stir the flour for a few minutes. Stir in the water and Worcestershire sauce and braise gently for 40 minutes. The filling is now ready, so add to this to your pastry-lined pudding bowl and cover with pastry, as mentioned opposite.

4. Steam the puddings for an hour. To steam, put the pudding (whilst still in it's bowl) in a large pan half filled with boiling water, cover and simmer. Check the water level regularly and top up wth more boiling water if required.

5. Turn out and serve.

BRESAOLA HOME CURED BEEF

Difficulty level 3

Bresaola is a homely introduction to charcuterie. The idea is that a lean joint of otherwise tough beef is marinated in a wine, sugar and salt brine, this having been cooked together beforehand. This recipe was given to me by Franco Taruschio when he owned the Walnut Tree and I worked at Gidleigh Park in Dartmoor.

There is no point in making four portions of this sort of thing. It keeps for months in any case. This recipe makes enough for about a dozen main course servings.

WHAT YOU'LL NEED... (SERVES 12)

- 2kg beef topside
- ½ bottle red wine
- 500g coarse salt
- 10g saltpetre
- 100g brown sugar
- 1 tablespoon crushed black peppercorns

- 1 tablespoon crushed juniper berries
- 1 sprig thyme
- 6 chillies
- 1 cinnamon stick
- 600ml water

HOW TO DO IT...

1. Combine all the brine ingredients – everything except the beef. Bring to the boil then allow the brine to cool completely.

2. Find the right sized container. You don't want any of the meat to stick out of the brine so a small bucket or similar would be good.

3. Leave for four days to marinate. Should any part of the joint nor be covered then turn the meat every day.

4. Lift from the brine then pat dry with kitchen paper. Wrap in muslin/cheesecloth then hang somewhere warm and dry for a fortnight or until quite firm when pressed. It is best hung away from the wall so that air can circulate. The outside will look awful but just trim it away. You should be left with a deep purple block that will keep for ages.

5. Slice thinly and dress with olive oil, parmesan shaving, herbs or whatever you heart desires.

Lamb Hamburger with Garlic and Pepper

Difficulty level 2

Interestingly I ate this, or something like it, at a fashionable restaurant in San Francisco. Americans, like many people, don't really go for lamb. Their loss...

What you'll need... (Serves 4)

- 700g minced lamb
- 12 garlic cloves
- 2 tablespoons cracked or crushed peppercorns
- 1 teaspoon olive oil
- 2 tomatoes – skinned de-seeded and chopped
- 1 tablespoon chopped coriander leaves
- 25g unsalted butter

How to do it...

1. Poach the garlic cloves in 300ml water until tender - about 15 minutes. Set the pan aside.

2. Season the minced lamb, quarter the mixture and press in to 4 patties.

3. Roll each patty in cracked black peppercorns.

4. Heat a frying pan. Brush the lamb patties with olive oil then cook briefly – about two minutes each side. They should still be rare.

5. Place each burger onto a warmed plate.

6. Deglaze the frying pan with the garlic and its cooking liquor.

7. Add the coriander, tomato and butter then shake the pan to amalgamate these ingredients.

8. Spoon over the lamb hamburgers and serve.

MEAT

The Gastronomical! guide to...

Faceless fish and bottom feeders

FISH

FISHY BUSINESS

According to The Oxford Encyclopaedia of Underwater Life (2005) there is no such thing as a 'fish'. This is because unlike mammals and birds, not all the creatures we call fish descend from the same common ancestor. It seems that most 'fish' are descended from four-legged land vertebrates, which obviously aren't fish at all. So, it's a term to use with caution. After all, in the 16th Century, seals, whales, crocodiles and even hippos were called fish and cuttlefish, starfish, crayfish, jellyfish and shellfish still are.

There are basically two groups of fish – those that fall into the 'oily' category and those that fall into the 'white' category. The difference between the two is – you guessed it – oil! White fish mainly have oil in their livers whereas oily fish have it in their tissues and in the belly cavity around the gut. Their fillets contain up to 30 percent oil, although this does vary both within and between species.

Whitefish are usually demersal fish which live on or near the seafloor, whereas oily fish are pelagic, living in the water away from the bottom.

Examples of oily fish are sardine, herring and anchovy, with larger examples including tuna, salmon and mackerel. Examples of whitefish are cod, haddock and flat fish.

WHY LEMON WITH FISH?

Many fish dishes, especially when eating out, arrive with the customary wedge of fresh lemon which is squeezed over the fish. When I queried a number of chefs as to why this was so, I didn't get a solid answer.

As a restaurateur, I had always assumed that the acidity in the lemon juice acted as a secondary form of cooking. After all, many places do like to serve fish just cooked. If this isn't to your taste then the acidity of lemon would cook the fish a little further on.

However, it would appear (after some detective work) that the custom of serving a slice of lemon with fish dates back to the Middle Ages when it was then believed that if a person accidentally swallowed a fish bone, the lemon juice would dissolve it.

But then others just say that the addition and squeezing of lemon over fish is popular in polite society to remove any fishy smell.

SPOTTING FRESH FISH AND SEAFOOD

We all know fish must be fresh to be eaten, but guaranteeing that is sometimes tricky. Here are a few tips on how to check it is fresh:

- Fish eyes should be clear and bulge slightly – and any that are cloudy or sunken indicates that the fish has been landed for a while and isn't at its freshest.

- Whole fish and filleted fish should have firm and shiny flesh. Ask the fishmonger if you can press the skin. If you press it with your finger and, when you let go, the flesh doesn't spring back up, this is another sure sign that the fish is not fresh.

- The gills on the fish should be a nice, bright red and free from slime - Slime in the gills could mean bacteria so avoid fish with slimy pale gills.

- The fish should smell mild, more like the sea than a fishy smell. If the fish smells fishy it has probably been there a while.

- Look out for yellow or brown discolouration on fillets of fish. This could indicate a lack of freshness.

- Is there liquid on the meat? If so, that liquid should be clear, not milky. Milky liquid on a fillet is the first stage of rot.

The best way to choose a live fish or crab or lobster is to look for, well, life. Is it scampering around in its tank? Swimming happily? Or is it sulking in a corner or hanging motionless and panting? If so, don't buy it. Lobsters and crabs starve themselves in tanks and often can be almost empty inside when you crack open one that's been imprisoned in a tank for weeks.

FISH

Scallops

Scallops are also sold out of their shells, so what you are looking for are 'dry packed' scallops, meaning they are not shipped and stored in brine. If you see scallops sitting in greying milky yak, leave them be. It is much better to buy frozen, vacuum-sealed scallops, which are perfectly good by the way, and much better than a smelly, wet-packed scallop. If you are lucky enough to have a good fishmonger nearby, you should be able to buy fresh scallops still in, or just out of, their shells - a real treat.

Shrimps

Shrimps are easy. Buy them whole and frozen. Why whole? This is because the shell protects the meat inside from the harshness of being frozen. Why frozen? Shrimp cook very rapidly and also rot very quickly. Cook from frozen.

Should you live near a shrimping region, or have access to truly magnificent fresh shrimp, buy them. But eat them the same day.

Part 3 - Faceless fish and bottom feeders   177

Shellfish

Try to buy seafood alive. Many types of shellfish such as scallops and mussels can be sold alive and should react to you but not by waving or smiling. Put them on the countertop and back away for a moment. Then tap the shell - it should close tighter than it was. Oysters are a little tough to do this with but clams and mussels will definitely react. You can always tell a dead shellfish after you've cooked them all. Dead ones do not open after being cooked. Throw them away immediately.

Octopus and Squid

Octopus and Squid are nearly always sold to the wholesaler pre-frozen so, unless you can buy fresh from a fishmonger, you should buy them frozen. Squid, or calamari, and its cousin, octopus, freeze well. Again, if you can buy them fresh it is best to do so.

They are such a treat and so nutritious and tasty. When buying fresh, the same rule applies as with fish. Look out for bright shiny eyes, and a wet nose!

Cooking well relies on a number of senses, one of the most important being your sense of smell. Learn to use your nose, not only when buying fish, but when buying fruit, cheese and vegetables. In fact, use your nose for everything and then learn to use it when you are cooking. Cooking aromas and noises can tell you a great deal about how your dish is coming along.

How to keep your Fish Fresh

A fish may be only a day old but if it is not stored correctly it might as well be a week old. Fish is always best used as soon as you get it. In fact, the sooner you can use it after purchasing the better. Keep the fish cool. Leaving a fish out for any length of time, even ten minutes, can cause it to lose freshness. For every hour a fish isn't kept cool, it loses a day of its shelf life.

The best way to get fresh fish is to find a reputable fishmonger. Ask them what's at its freshest. Get to know your fishmonger and purchase from him, or her, regularly. Most will be happy of the regular custom and will point you in the right direction for the best catch. As soon as you choose your fish ask your fishmonger to gut and gill it for you, so any bacteria held in these areas cannot permeate into the flesh of the fish. Then keep it cool in the fridge and use as soon as possible.

Look at your surroundings. A good fish shop should not reek! If you walk into a fish shop or market and it stinks, leave.

WHAT IS SUSTAINABILITY
– AND SHOULD WE BE BOTHERED?

Absolutely, the answer is yes.

Our oceans and seas have been overfished in recent years to a massive extent with nearly 75% of the world's fisheries over fished or fully fished. Basically we are taking too many fish from our oceans and destroying ecosystems (the food chains and circumstances that other species and plants need to survive) in the process - if we carry on like this many fish stocks will collapse and the marine ecosystem may be irreparably damaged.

Fishermen have quotas in Europe on how much can be caught, at what size and of which species. Discarding is an EU (European Union) practice on fishing that insists that any excess to the allowed quota, any under or over size fish must be thrown back into the sea. Dead. The practice of discarding however has been reviewed and will be phased out over the next few years to be replaced by a 'landing obligation' meaning all fish caught must be kept on board then counted against the allowed quota, fish that are too small will not be marked for human consumption and can be returned to the sea.

What a waste.

Sustainable fish and seafood refers to species which either remains plentiful in our seas and oceans, or are farmed to protect them from becoming endangered. Mackerel is an example of a fish currently classed as being sustainable. The classification covers both saltwater and freshwater types of fish.

It isn't difficult

Buying sustainable fish is gradually becoming easier because there is now clear labelling that marks out products as good to buy from certified sustainable fisheries. The Marine Stewardship Council have introduced identifiable blue labels for packaging and people can also find certified suppliers online.

So what can you do to help? Encourage your parents to only buy sustainable fish and seafood. Explore the other varied and wonderful alternatives. Our sea are full of delicious and nutritious species, here are a few recommendations:

Pollack: Found throughout the north-east Atlantic, pollack is championed as the best substitute for Cod and Haddock.

Megrim: A common flatfish found in shelf seas throughout the north-east Atlantic, megrim are members of the sole family. Around 90% of Britain's Megrim catch is exported to the continent.

Mackerel: A fast-swimming species belonging to a group of fish related to the tuna. It's an oily fish with a distinctive flavour. Stocks are healthy, except in the North Sea.

Lemon sole: The fishery for lemon sole is largely unregulated. Taken as by-catch in trawl fisheries, only stocks in Norwegian and North Seas are subject to mixed quota restrictions

White Fish

There are many different species of white fish such as plaice, cod, monkfish, john dory, haddock, sole and skate. These fish are much less oily that the 'oily' ones we've talked about and often have a lighter more subtle flavour. Let's look at the most common fish we eat.

Cod

Cod has been important since the Vikings. Norwegians travelled with dried cod and helped develop a dried cod market across Southern Europe which lasted for more than 1,000 years. Cod meat is moist and flaky when cooked and white in colour.

Mullet

Mullet are found across the world in tropical and subtropical waters including the bays and estuaries on Florida's Atlantic and Gulf Coasts. The body of the mullet is elongated and rather stout. It's dark bluish on the top and silver along the sides and has a small mouth with closely set teeth and widely separately dorsal fins. It's average weight is around 1kg, but can be in excess of 3kg.

Mullet swim in large schools and are commonly seen jumping out of the water, which is why they can be called jumping mullet. This makes it easy for fishermen to spot the fish even in the dark.

The mullet is considered a vegetarian and is the only fish that has a gizzard, much like a chicken, that is used to grind up and digest plant material.

It is also a really dodgy hairstyle favoured by Australian and New Zealand men and women – though some really bad ones have been spotted in Devon.

John Dory

Another freaky looking fish, which is also known as Saint Pierre. It is a flatfish, oval in shape with the wildest looking spines on the dorsal fin and olive-yellow in colour. It is a deep-sea fish with a large body which has a large dark spot on it – some say the dark spot is used to flash an 'evil eye', others that it is the thumb print of Saint Peter. To help avoid danger, it has a large mouth and large eyes which give it bifocal vision and depth perception, which are important to avoid predators.

The john dory grows to a maximum size of 65 cm and 3kg in weight. Its eyes are near the top of its head and it is a poor swimmer. The john dory usually gets its food by stalking it then shooting out a tube in its mouth to capture its prey. It eats a variety of fish, especially schooling fish, such as sardines. Their predators are sharks and other large bony fish. They are normally solitary. Fishy-no-mates.

Plaice

Plaice is a flat fish about 60cm in length (although some can measure one metre and weigh up to 7kg) with a pattern of brown spots on its body. It is very commonly found on the sandy and muddy bottoms of the European shelf, usually at depths of between 10 and 50 metres, where they tend to burrow in sediment during day time and remain stationary for long periods.

The most obvious characteristic of the flatfish is their asymmetry, with both eyes lying on the same side of the head in the adult fish. In some families, the eyes are always on the right side of the body. In others, they are always on the left! Plaice lie on the seabed on their left side, while turbot lie on their right side. They are able to survive low salt concentrations and have on occasion been found living in freshwater. They can live up to 50 years old! Plaice is often used as the 'fish' in fish and chip shops.

Monkfish

Monkfish are genuinely amongst the most disgusting looking fish you will ever see! It has an enormous, flat head with a large mouth and very sharp teeth. The head makes up approximately 75% of the body and is as wide as the fish is long. The only bit of the monkfish you can eat is the tail meat (apart from the liver) – because apart from its massive ugly head, that is all there is! Having said that, this bit of fish meat is amongst the most delicious to eat. Its texture is similar to that of lobster meat, and in fact used to be called 'poor man's lobster'. Nowadays though it can often be more expensive than lobster to buy.

They are a bottom-dwelling and feeding fish. As part of the anglerfish family of fish, the monkfish uses a piece of skin at the top of its head to lure in fish and capture them. Monkfish can grow up to 1.2m and weigh as much as 22kg. Fishermen generally remove the head and only bring in the tail. The liver is used in the preparation of certain types of sushi and sashimi.

Oily Fish

Sardine is a term used to describe around 20 different small, soft-boned, oily fish. In Britain, they are usually pilchards.

They are found in coastal subtropical and temperate waters. They grow really quickly reaching half their full size in about a year and their full length in 4 years. Whilst they can grow to over 30cm, they seldom grow longer than 23cm.

Sardines are filter feeders, sieving plankton from the water as it passes between their gills.

An adult dusky shark was once found with 621 sardines in its stomach.

Some people believe that if you dream of sardines you have troubles ahead. Maybe a disagreement among relatives?

Sardines were named after the Mediterranean island of Sardinia, where they were once found in abundance.

Tuna

There are 48 species of Tuna – the best known are yellowfin, bluefin and albacore. The word tuna dates back only to 1880 in print.

Tuna have been fished from the warm, temperate parts of the Mediterranean Sea, the Pacific, Atlantic, and Indian Oceans since ancient times. Tuna has a stronger, more robust flavour than whitefish.

Tuna swim at a steady rate of nine miles per hour, and they never stop moving. It is estimated that a 15-year-old tuna will have travelled a million miles in its lifetime. And tuna are fast, reaching speeds of around 55 miles an hour. To keep this kind of speed up, tuna has to eat a huge amount of food, the equivalent of up to 25% of its body weight daily.

The majority of the commercial tuna harvest comes from California. Most of the catch is destined never to be eaten fresh and instead ends up in a tin. Either way, tuna is very good for you and tastes delicious – especially fresh and raw!

Name that tuna

✓ The albacore tuna is a silvery blue colour, shaped like a torpedo and can grow up to a metre in length. Nicknamed the 'chicken of the sea', the albacore tuna has a delicious, pale, meaty flesh. Albacore of a similar size travel together in schools, which can be can be up to 19 miles wide.

✓ The Atlantic bluefin tuna is one of the largest and fastest fish in the world. Their bodies are also shaped like streamlined torpedoes, which gives them extra speed and endurance.

✓ The Atlantic bluefin tuna has a voracious appetite, which helps it grow to a whopping 1.8m in length.

✓ Atlantic bluefins are warm-blooded; a rare trait among fish. They are equally at home in cold waters as in tropical waters. Basically they raise their body temperature with muscular activity.

✓ Bluefins swim back and forth from North America to Europe several times a year.

FISH

Can I see your ticket please?

Salmon once told me...

Salmon find their home waters by sense of smell which is as keen as a dog's. They also rely on ocean currents, tides and the gravitational pull of the moon to navigate their way through the ocean back to the stream or river where they were born.

Sometimes, for a salmon to get back to the area where it was born, it has to jump over a waterfall or dam. It can take a salmon a whole day of trying to jump a waterfall before is it successful. In Scotland, the highest jump a salmon has been known to make is at the Orrin Falls in Rosshire, where the salmon has to jump over 3.7 metres! Most salmon can be seen trying to jump at waterfalls in autumn time. Adult salmon stop feeding when they come back to the river - sometimes for over a year.

Salmon meat shows growth rings like a tree and periods of rapid growth during summer months is clearly discernable from smaller winter growth rings. Freshwater growth rings are usually dense and ocean growth rings are widely spaced, indicating faster growth rates at sea.

Salmon Trivia

- Usually we measure the weight of a salmon in pounds (remember, one kilogram in weight is equivalent to 2.2 lbs).

- The largest salmon on record caught by fishing rod in the UK was caught on the River Tay. It was caught by Miss Georgina Ballantyne and weighed a massive 64lbs (29kg)!

- Some fishermen are prepared to spend hundreds of pounds a day to catch a salmon for sport.

- Salmon are very sensitive to pollution - they require very cool, clean water. If you have salmon in your river, you probably have a clean river!

MACKEREL

Mackerel is a common name for a number of different of fish. They are a slim, cylindrical shape, as opposed to tuna which are deeper-bodied.

It takes a mackerel around 7 years to reach 450g in weight and they can live for 25 years. A female mackerel lays about one million eggs at a time.

Mackerel are found in all tropical and temperate seas. Most live offshore but a few, like the Spanish mackerel, enter bays and can be caught near bridges and piers.

Eel be coming round the mountain...

Well, no, not actually. Eel are usually found in shallow waters and burrow into sandy beds forming eel pits. They swim upstream into rivers, returning to the sea to breed.

Ranging from 5cm – 4 metres in length, with weights from 30g to 25kg, eel meat is high in potassium, calcium and vitamin A. The meat is considered firm and rich tasting and unlike many other types of fish it takes well to stewing. Eel also works extremely well when smoked.

The majority of al eel eaten, around 70%, is consumed in Japan where it is vastly popular, though nowadays it seems to be appearing on many a UK restaurant menu.

Eel Trivia

- At one time, eels were so plentiful in the River Thames that nets were set as far up as London. This provided a cheap, nutritious and available foodstuff to the poorer population of the city.

- The dish, jellied eels, is thought to have originated in the East End of London in the 18th Century. The dish is made of chopped eels, cooked in a spiced stock and left to go cold and jellied. It is then eaten cold with bread and butter.

- Eel blood is poisonous to humans. However the cooking and digestive process destroys the toxic protein, making it safe.

- Eels are mostly nocturnal.

- Baby eels, called elvers, travel from the ocean where they are born, to inland waters where they intend to mature into adults. Once popular in the West of England, elvers are a delicacy and can sometimes be as expensive as caviar.

Trout pout

A close relative of salmon, trout has three common varieties; brown trout, rainbow trout and sea trout.

A fact that many of you may not know is that the brown and sea trout are, actually, the same species. During the course of the brown trout's life, nature decides that a proportion of them will be migratory. This means they take a trip to the sea and spend their days there, rather than in a river, returning to rivers only to spawn. Brown trout are characterised by their dullish coloured skin with large black and red/orange spots.

The rainbow trout, pretty with its silvery skin, which radiates blue, green and pink highlights when lit by the sun's rays is native only to the rivers and lakes of North America. However, over time, the value of the rainbow trout as a game fish, not to mention as a delicious catch, has resulted in its introduction throughout the world.

Trout meat, regardless of the variety, is extremely versatile and delicious. It produces oily meat, high in omega 3 and vitamin D.

Trout trivia

- Trout can change colour, they get darker when aggressive and lighter when submissive.
- Brown trout have between 38 & 42 pairs of chromosomes, humans have 23.
- Trout do not laugh when being tickled, that's an old poaching method.
- With a brain the size of a pea, the trout are pretty good at outwitting fishermen.
- The largest species of trout, the caspia trout, has been reported to weigh in at a whopping 51kg.

Yin and yang

Trout can change colour, they get darker when aggressive
and lighter when submissive.

Part 3 - Faceless fish and bottom feeders

SCARY PIKERS

Often feared by fishermen for their bad tempers and sharp teeth, pike are usually found in rivers, reservoirs and lakes. They average at around 130cm long, the largest caught on record caught being 180cm.

The pike's body has yellow and green markings, forming a clever underwater camouflage which, along with its sharp eyesight and razor like teeth, all help the fish to succeed as a hunter.

Considered too bony to be cooked, it can be tricky to prepare - but it isn't impossible - and the earthy, rich meat is high in selenium, vitamin B12 and protein.

PIKE TRIVIA

- ✅ Pike can live for up to 18 years.
- ✅ Evidence has been found that Romans used to eat pike.
- ✅ Large pike can eat frogs, mice, small birds and even baby ducklings!
- ✅ Pike can also be cannibalistic, eating smaller pike.
- ✅ Fantastic hunters, pike sit, wait and then strike!

Bottom Feeders - Lobsters

A lobster is made up of these simple parts: thorax, tail, flipper, crusher claw, pincher claw, legs and antennae. If, for some reason, you're eager to know if you're about to eat a male or female lobster, all you need to do is look behind the legs for a small pair of appendages on the underside of the lobster. If these appendages are hard and boney, it's a male. If they are soft and feathery, you've got a female.

Lobster blood is clear and turns an opaque white when cooked. It has no flavour and is perfectly fine to eat. The green stuff you may find is called 'tomalley', and is the equivalent of a liver and pancreas for the lobster. Many people consider tomalley to be a delicacy.

Move over Dr Who

It is not just Dr Who that can grow a new hand. Lobsters can also regenerate! They can grown new legs, claws and antennae. In fact they can amputate their own claws and legs to escape from danger. Sometimes they can drop a claw for no reason at all. In a punch-up, a really aggressive lobster will tear the claw off an opponent.

Believe it or not lobsters are either right or left-handed. You don't tell this by which side they hold their knife or fork, or even by which hand they write with but by looking at their claws. One claw is sharp and used for cutting, the other is bony and used for crushing. Lobsters that have their heavy 'crusher' claw on the right are considered right-handed and the others are left-handed. Some lobsters can be ambidextrous and favour the claw that is the largest.

Lobsters come in a variety of colours from blue-green, a dark reddish-brown, yellow, to white, orange and red. Albino lobsters are the only ones that don't turn red when cooked. When lobsters are cooked, all other pigments are masked except for the underlying red colour - this is why all lobsters are the same colour when you eat them.

Today lobster is considered an expensive luxury but there used to be so many of them lying around that they could be collected by hand at low tide and were considered cheap food for servants. Some servants, in fact, insisted that employers sign a contract stating they would not have to eat lobster more than three times a week! We should be so lucky today!

Screaming Lobsters Batman!

Although lobsters have to be cooked alive they definitely do not scream! They have no vocal cords so can't even have a quick chat over a coral fence. The sound of 'screaming' you hear when you drop a lobster into boiling water is actually steam escaping from the shell as the lobster cooks. If you're worried about hurting a lobster, begin to cook it in cold water instead of hot. As the temperature rises, it will put the lobster to sleep, so will laying it on its back for a few minutes.

You must never cook a dead lobster – unless it has been frozen. Lobsters have an enzyme that breaks down their flesh as soon as they die so that it becomes mushy and nasty to eat. It will also make you pretty sick! Lobsters are bottom-feeders, which means that all they eat is rubbish and dirt from the sea bed. If you found a dead one you would not know what it died from – so best leave it to rest in peace.

LOBSTER TRIVIA

✓ On average, lobsters take 6 to 8 years to reach a legal catch size of 1 lb (453g).

✓ The largest lobster ever reported was 20 kg (44 lb), estimated to be between 40 and 65 years old.

✓ Lobsters usually hunt for food at night. They eat fish, crabs, clams, snails, sea stars, mussels and sea urchins.

✓ By nature, lobsters are not cannibalistic, except when held in crowded conditions then they will turn on each other.

✓ To escape from enemies, lobsters swim backwards by flipping their tail.

✓ The lobster's body has 19 parts, each covered by a section of the shell. The shell is thin and soft where the parts join, so lobsters can bend their body and move about.

Like dolphins, lobsters use complicated signals to establish
social relationships. They sometimes walk hand-in-hand, the
old leading the young.

Bottom Feeders - Crabs

Like lobsters, crabs must be cooked alive! They have the same kind of enzyme that destroys its flesh as soon as it dies and pretty soon it can be very toxic. The RSPCA recommends that you place your live crab in the draw of your freezer for a couple of hours before dropping it into boiling water – this will make it unconscious. And unaware.

One good thing about a crab is that it is very unlikely to ever bite you. Pinch you yes – but bite? Never. That's because the crab's teeth are in its stomach.

Crabs

There are over 5,000 species of crabs in the whole world but only 4,500 species are true crabs - the other 500 crabs are hermit crabs which are not 'true' crabs.

When you think about it a crab is very similar to a Dalek. Hard and crusty on the outside, soft and squidgy on the inside. Crabs, like Dr Who and lobsters, can also regenerate! In fact, only the claws of the stone crab are eaten. So, if a crabber catches a stone crab, they'll tear off the claws and throw the rest of the crab back into sea where it will regenerate the claws within 18 months. That's a long time without arms!

Male crabs with one large claw use this to attract females. This claw is not used for defence or to attack but to lure the females for mating purposes

Pea Crab

The pea crab is the smallest crab. It lives inside oyster shells and can be less than 1.5mm long.

Japanese Spider crab

The Japanese spider crab is the world's largest crab, and can reach 3.6 metres from leg tip to leg tip! That is probably more than twice the length of your dad lying down. There is an unconfirmed record of one measuring about 6 metres across. That's about 3 dads and a little sister lying head to toe.

Spider crabs are fairly common and live 300 to 400 metres down in the sea. They can live for up to 100 years and are sometimes referred to as living fossils.

Blue Crabs

America has more varieties of crabs than anywhere else in the world and by far the most popular is the blue crab.

While the female blue crab is in her molted state (soft shell crab), the male blue crab will protect her. The female however, will devour any male that comes along her way.

A tagged blue crab was recorded swimming 35 miles in 48 hours!

Red King Crabs

Red king crabs are a large species, weighing on average between 2.7kg to 4.5kg (about the weight of a good size newborn baby). The largest king crab on record weighed 10.9kg and had a leg span of almost 1.5m.

The crabs are caught in metal pots that are baited with minced herring, sardines or cod, before being dropped 120m below the surface. As crabs do not migrate in the same pattern each year, fishermen must rely on their experience and intuition to find the best locations to fish.

Mitten crabs

Mitten crabs are is a delicacy in Chinese and Japanese restaurants and are eaten raw, preferably with its reproductive organs swollen!

If you see a crab in freshwater it is almost certain to be a mitten crab.

Politician Peter Mandelson was once jokingly likened to a mitten crab by Deputy Prime Minister John Prescott during a photocall on the Thames.

The mature mitten crab is the size of a dinner plate when its legs are extended (the body is around 8cm wide and the legs about 12cm long)

CRAB TRIVIA

✓ Crabs are typically known to walk sideways. This is because of the articulation of the legs which makes a sidelong stride easier. However, some crabs prefer to walk forwards or backwards.

✓ Crabs communicate by drumming - not like Dave Grohl or Phil Collins though. They use their pincers, which they wave about a lot. They can work together as a team, for example to find food and safety for their families, or a safe place for a female to lay her eggs, but they also fight a lot. Especially over girls.

✓ Fishermen are only allowed to harvest adult male crabs. All females and juveniles must be thrown back.

✓ If a crab dies in the boat's holding tank, it emits toxins that can poison the others. One dead crab can wipe out the entire catch!

✓ Fresh water, warm water or bad water circulation in a boat's holding tank all have the potential to kill crabs. In fact, stagnant water will kill crabs faster than leaving them out of the water.

Prawn to be wild...

The name 'prawn' is commonly used to describe a species of shellfish that is part of the lobster family. Prawns have minuscule claws and bodies shaped a little like tiny lobsters. They are 15 to 20 centimetres long and have pale red bodies deepening to dark red tails. Their meat has a sweet delicate flavour. Included in this definition of 'prawn' are Dublin Bay prawn, Danish lobster, langoustine and Florida lobsterette.

Freshwater prawns are prawns that migrate from saltwater to freshwater to spawn (lay eggs). They look like a cross between a shrimp and a lobster. Their abdomens are narrower and legs are longer than those of shrimp.

Prawn trivia

The earliest fossil prawns were found in rocks in Madagascar that are 250 million years old.

Flamingos owe their pink or reddish colour to the rich sources of carotenoid pigments in the algae and small crustaceans that they eat.

HOW IS A SQUID LIKE A SNAIL?

They're both molluscs, one of the major groups of invertebrates (animals without backbones).

Squid are marine cephalopod (ocean mollusc) and there are about 500 species of them. As an invertebrate, a squid has no bones. A feather-shaped blade helps support the body. It is made of chitin, like your fingernails. Cartilage, which is tough, gristle-like tissue, surrounds and protects a squid's brain.

They have 3 hearts, a large one that pumps blood around their body (like ours) and two smaller one that feed their gills. The hearts are greenish in colour. Apart from three hearts (that's one more than Doctor Who), these creatures really are strange. They have eight arms plus two tentacles at the head end and also have a beak.

Squid have the biggest eyes (for their size) in the animal kingdom – they are on either side of the head and contain a hard lens. The lens is focused through movement, much like the lens of a camera or telescope, rather than changing shape as the in the human eye. But what they have in eyesight they lose in hearing – it appears that either the squid is limited in this area or no one has ever said that much interesting to them to make them bothered to respond. They probably would be quite chatty if they could talk though because they exhibit high intelligence (for an invertebrate). For example, groups of Humboldt squid hunt as a team, using their own form of communication.

The way they get about is quite interesting – they propel. Here's how they do it – first they suck in water then they contract their muscles and jet out the water.

Most squid are no more than 60cms long – that's 24 inches – about the width of an average cooker. Giant squid though can get to 13 metres (or 46 feet – about the size of your average power boat).

In English-speaking countries we usually know squid by the Italian word calamari. The body can be stuffed whole, cut into flat pieces or sliced into rings. The arms, tentacles and ink are also edible. Squid is a good food source for zinc, selenium, copper and vitamin B12.

FISH

WHAT HAS A FOOT BUT NO LEGS?
– A MUSSEL!

Both the male and female of this edible species have beards (yes, beards) and the only way to tell them apart is that the inside of the female is orange in colour, while the male is paler and a greyish white. Not appreciated for their looks, we have been ignoring their rather ugly appearance for thousands of years because they taste delicious.

The name mussel is used for several families of clams but for our purpose we are referring to the common mussel. In most marine mussels the shell is longer than it is wide, being wedge-shaped. The outside colour of the shell is often dark blue, blackish, or brown, while the interior is silvery and shiny.

The mussel's external shell is composed of two hinged halves or 'valves'. The valves are joined together on the outside by a ligament, and are closed when necessary by strong internal muscles. Mussel shells carry out a variety of functions, including support for soft tissues and protection from predators.

The foot

Mussels have a large organ called a foot. In freshwater mussels, this foot is large, muscular, and generally hatchet-shaped. It is used to pull the animal through sand, gravel, or silt. In marine mussels, the foot is smaller, tongue-like in shape, with a groove on it. This forms extremely tough, strong and elastic threads (also known as the beard – mentioned earlier) that fixes the mussel to its domain. The thread is also sometimes used by mussels as a defensive measure, to tether predatory molluscs that invade mussel beds, immobilising them and starving them to death.

Mussels are filter feeders. They feed on plankton and other microscopic sea creatures which are in seawater. Some people avoid eating mussels because they think they also feed on waste and dirt in the sea making them dirty and unhealthy. In fact mussels are full of zinc and selenium.

In Ireland, mussels can be boiled and seasoned with vinegar. The 'bray' or boiling water is consumed as a supplementary hot drink.

Mussels can be smoked, boiled, steamed, roasted, barbecued or fried in butter.

As with all shellfish, except shrimps, mussels should be checked to ensure they are still alive just before they are cooked. There are enzymes that quickly break down the meat and make them unpalatable and sometimes dangerous after dying. An easy trick to know is that live mussels, when in the air, will shut tightly when disturbed. So don't have your nose too close to that live mussel when you peer inside.

A BASIC COOKING GUIDELINE

Mackerel – Pan-fry, grill, BBQ

Salmon and trout – Pan-fry, poach, steam, bake, grill, BBQ

Sardines – Grill, BBQ, pan-fry, bake

Tuna, shark and swordfish – Grill, BBQ, pan-fry, bake, stew, braise

Bass and mullet - Poach, steam, bake, BBQ

Cod and Haddock – Pan-fry, deep-fry, grill, poach, bake

Monkfish – Pan-fry, bake, grill, BBQ

John Dory – Poach, grill, pan-fry

Plaice – Pan-fry, poach, deep-fry, grill, steam, bake

Skate - Grill, steam, bake, pan-fry, deep-fry

Turbot – Steam, poach, pan-fry, grill, bake – wrapped or unwrapped

FISH RECIPES

IN THIS SECTION…

RECIPES FROM MARCUS WAREING

FISH

HOW TRICKY ARE THE RECIPES? LOOK OUT FOR THESE…

Difficulty level 1

Difficulty level 2

Difficulty level 3

Homemade hake fish fingers

Difficulty level 1

What you'll need... (Serves 4)

- 600g hake
- 50g plain flour
- 1 egg
- 175g fine white breadcrumbs

How to do it...

1. Cut the fish into 8 thick and even pieces. Dust each piece of fish lightly with the flour.

2. Beat the egg and pour into a shallow dish. Place the breadcrumbs onto a flat plate.

3. Using your fingers, dip each piece of fish first in the beaten egg, then in the breadcrumbs making sure they are evenly covered. Put in the fridge for 25 minutes.

4. Half-fill a deep frying pan with vegetable oil and heat until very hot. Add half the hake and fry for 3-4 minutes, turning once or twice until the breadcrumb coating is crisp and light golden in colour. Remove and drain on a clean tea towel.

5. Cook the rest of the hake in the same way.

6. Serve immediately, with salad, chips or (our favourite) in a sandwich with mayonnaise.

Whether it's mayo and lettuce, or loaded with ketchup, you can't beat a fish finger sarnie.

Grilled sardines

Difficulty level 1

What you'll need… (Serves 4)

- 12 fresh sardines, ask the fishmonger to gut and clean them
- 1 tablespoon chopped parsley
- 1 tablespoon chopped chives
- 1 tablespoon chopped tarragon
- 1 tablespoon chopped mint
- 1 tablespoon Dijon mustard
- Juice of ½ lemon
- Salt and cracked black pepper
- Olive oil

How to do it…

1. In a small bowl mix all the herbs, mustard and lemon juice.

2. Wash the sardines in cold water and then pat dry with kitchen paper.

3. Open up the fish up and sprinkle some salt and cracked black pepper inside.

4. Divide the mustard and herb mixture between the sardines, spoon inside the cavity of each fish.

5. Brush the outside of the sardines very lightly with olive oil.

6. Place the sardines underneath the grill and cook for 2/3 minutes on each side to brown.

7. Turn the grill down and cook for a further 5 minutes. You could also use something called a griddle pan, which you would heat on the hob.

8. Serve with brown bread and butter.

FISH

Cod Mornay

What you'll need... (Serves 4)

- 350g cod loin
- 180g of spinach
- 2 large maris piper potatoes sliced thinly
- 3 shallots – finely chopped
- 250ml milk

- 50g of butter
- Salt and pepper
- Pinch of nutmeg
- 1 slice of bread whizzed up into breadcrumbs

Difficulty level 1

For the sauce:

- 75g butter
- 75g plain flour

- 170g mature cheddar cheese
- 180ml of whole milk, plus 250ml of the milk used for poaching the fish

How to do it...

1. Take a large frying pan, heat it up then add the breadcrumbs and cook until they start to colour. Set aside onto a cold plate.

2. Now using the same frying pan, throw in the butter. When the butter starts to bubble, add the chopped shallots. Cook the shallots for five minutes or until they become soft – you don't want them to colour.

3. Add the spinach and season with salt, pepper and a quarter of a teaspoon of nutmeg. Turn frequently with a wooden spoon, once the spinach has wilted (about 2 minutes) take the pan off the heat.

4. Get another pan. Add the 250ml of milk, bring to the boil, and then gently put in the fish. Add four or five twists of black pepper from a mill.

5. When the fish is cooked, remove it from the milk. It's quite simple to know when the fish is cooked - the flesh will start to flake (fall apart) easily. Do not throw the milk away.

6. Put the cod onto a plate and break it up using a fork.

7. Peel and slice the potatoes as thin as you can.

8. Lay the potatoes in a shallow dish with a little water. Cover with cling film, make a couple of holes and pop it into the microwave for two minutes. We are cooking them very slightly as they may not get cooked enough in the oven. However, we do not want to overcook the fish.

9. Taking a saucepan, add the butter. When melted, add the flour. Cook for a minute, stirring with a wooden spoon.

10. A little bit at a time, add the milk you have saved from poaching the fish in. Stir all the time.

11. Add the 180ml of milk, stirring continuously on the heat until the sauce bubbles and begins to thicken.

12. Turn down to a simmer and cook for a few minutes until your sauce is creamy and not lumpy.

13. Remove the sauce from the heat. Add most of the cheddar cheese but save a small handful for sprinkling on top.

14. Take a medium sized gratin dish or similar:

15. Firstly do a layer of the cheese sauce, then a layer of potatoes.

16. Then a layer of spinach, then another layer of potatoes.

17. Then a layer of all of the flaky fish.

18. Cover with the rest of the sauce. Sprinkle over breadcrumbs and remaining cheese.

19. Bake in the oven at 180°C for 35 minutes.

20. Serve with lightly boiled green beans or broccoli.

Fish Kebabs

What you'll need... (Serves 4)

Difficulty level 1

- ✓ 1 green pepper
- ✓ 450g pollock
- ✓ 16 cherry tomatoes
- ✓ 12 seedless grapes
- ✓ 8 button mushrooms
- ✓ 8 bay leaves
- ✓ Lemon juice
- ✓ 2 teaspoons chopped fresh tarragon

How to do it...

1. Chop pepper into rough-sized pieces of about 3cm square. Put into a saucepan, just cover with water and simmer for 10 minutes. Drain.

2. Dice your fish into even sized 3cm cubes.

3. Take your skewers and thread the fish, tomatoes, grapes, mushrooms, pieces of pepper and bay leaves.

4. Sprinkle the kebabs with lemon juice and tarragon.

5. Heat the grill, or place on the BBQ. Cook for 10 minutes or until the fish is cooked, turning often to make sure it is cooked evenly on all sides.

6. Serve with salad or boiled new potatoes and your choice of green vegetable.

Sweet 'n' Spicy Mackerel

What you'll need... (Serves 4)

- 2 whole mackerel, ask your fishmonger to clean and take off the head
- 1 carrot
- 1 stick of celery
- 2 inch piece of ginger
- 2 tablespoons honey
- 1 tablespoon white wine vinegar
- 1 tablespoon soya sauce
- Salt and pepper

How to do it...

1. Finely julienne (cut into matchstick-sized strips) the carrot, ginger and celery.
2. Place the fish onto a large piece of greased baking foil.
3. Very gently slightly warm the honey in a saucepan.
4. Brush the mackerel with the honey.
5. Put the celery, carrot and ginger strips on the fish.
6. Pour over the soy sauce and vinegar.
7. Lift the sides of the foil up and fold to make a watertight parcel. Place on a baking tray in a oven preheated to 170°C, cook for 30 minutes and serve.

FISH

Super quick to make and full of flavour - you've got no excuses!

Trout with Lemon & Caper butter

Difficulty level 2

'Grenobloise' is a classic French sauce, composed of capers, brown butter or 'beurre noisette' and lemon. This is a classic dish from Grenoble, a city in south-eastern France. ' La Truite Grenobloise'

What you'll need... (Serves 2)

- ☑ **2 large trout fillets**
- ☑ **1 tablespoon olive oil**
- ☑ **1 tablespoon salted butter**
- ☑ **½ lemon, segmented, then diced**
- ☑ **1 tablespoon fresh lemon juice**
- ☑ **½ tablespoon capers**

How to do it...

1. Rinse the trout in cold water and pat very dry with a clean tea towel.

2. Drizzle some olive oil on to an empty flat plate. Season the oil with salt and pepper.

3. Place a large frying pan on the hob and heat.

4. Place the fillets onto the oil on the plate and turn, making sure they are well covered.

5. Place the fillets skin side down into the frying pan. When the skin is light golden brown and crispy you can turn them over and cook for another minute or two. Put the fish onto a plate. Keep warm.

6. Turn the heat under the pan right down.

7. After a few seconds, add the butter to the same (not washed) pan.

8. Return the pan to a low heat and cook until the butter is brown.

9. At this stage, your butter is known to be 'noisette'.

10. You should be able to smell a pleasant nutty aroma.

11. Remove pan from heat, add the diced lemon segments and juice.

12. Return to low heat and add the capers.

13. Spoon the juices over the fish. Serve with boiled new potatoes and green beans.

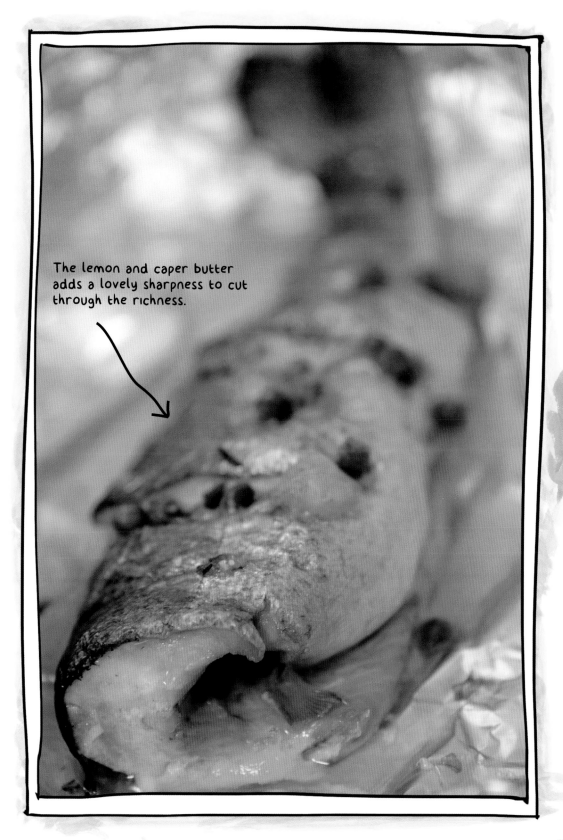

The lemon and caper butter adds a lovely sharpness to cut through the richness.

Blackened Tuna Steaks

Difficulty level 1

What you'll need... (Serves 4)

 4 fresh tuna steaks

 Cajun seasoning

 Olive oil

 Knob of butter

How to do it...

1. Put the olive oil & butter into a frying pan. Turn on to medium-high heat.

2. Pour the cajun seasoning into a shallow baking tray. The tray should be wide enough to fit each tuna steak when laid flat.

3. Lay the tuna steak down on top of the cajun seasoning. Press down on the tuna steak to really make the seasoning stick.

4. Flip the tuna steak over and coat the other side with the cajun seasoning the same way. Repeat for each tuna steak.

5. Place the tuna steaks into the frying pan once the oil has begun to smoke.

6. Cook until the underside is blackened, which usually takes between 3 to 4 minutes. Flip the tuna steak over and repeat the cooking process on the other side.

7. Serve with green salad.

Tinned Pilchards in Puff Pastry

Difficulty level 1

What you'll need… (Serves 1)

- 1 tin pilchards in tomato sauce
- Ready-made puff pastry
- Rocket leaves
- Shaved parmesan cheese
- Olive oil
- Rock salt
- 1 egg for egg wash
- Preheat oven to 180°C

How to do it…

1. Open the can of pilchards and remove the fish. Lay on a plate.

2. Roll out the puff pastry to 1cm thickness. Brush with egg wash.

3. Lay the pilchards side by side across the centre of the pastry leaving a nice border around.

4. Bake in a preheated oven at 180°C until the pastry has risen around the fish and turned golden brown.

5. Remove from oven and put on plate.

6. Sprinkle rocket leaves and shaved parmesan on top.

7. Drizzle a little olive oil and grind a little rock salt over.

8. Perfect with a salad or as a starter.

FISH

Tuna & Sweetcorn Pizza

Difficulty level 1

What you'll need... (Serves 4)

- ☑️ 1 large ready-made pizza base or 2 smaller bases
- ☑️ 1 jar tomato and herb pizza topping
- ☑️ 1 large tin tuna in spring water, drained
- ☑️ 12 pitted olives, green or black, drained
- ☑️ 2 small or one medium red onion, finely sliced
- ☑️ 1 tin sweetcorn, drained
- ☑️ 100g grated mature cheddar cheese
- ☑️ 2 tablespoons ketchup
- ☑️ 1 tablespoon butter

How to do it...

1. In a shallow frying pan add the butter and onion and caramelise. This is when you cook to go a lovely golden brown, which shows the onions sugars have been released.

2. Add the jar of tomato topping and the ketchup and mix thoroughly, then remove from heat.

3. Spread the tomato topping evenly over the pizza bases.

4. Sprinkle over the tuna, olives and sweetcorn.

5. Cover with the grated cheddar.

6. Bake for 20 minutes in an oven preheated to 200°C.

7. Leave to rest for 2 minutes before slicing.

WHITEBAIT

Whitebait are young fish. In Europe the term applies to young herring, but in other parts of the world it is used for similar fish of other species. The whole whitebait is edible. The entire fish is eaten including head and fins.

Difficulty level 2

Whitebait first started appearing on English menus all the way back in 1612, however the fish failed to reach 'fashionable' heights on restaurant menus until around 1780. In those days, both the fishermen who caught and chefs who cooked whitebait, believed that it was a separate type of fish altogether, not just a baby herring.

WHAT YOU'LL NEED... (SERVES 4)

- ✔ **1kg whitebait**
- ✔ **Plain flour**
- ✔ **Salt and pepper**
- ✔ **Vegetable oil for deep frying**
- ✔ **Lemon wedges**

FISH

HOW TO DO IT...

1. Rinse the fish and pat dry.

2. Sieve the flour into a bowl and season with salt & pepper.

3. Drop the whitebait into the flour and using your fingers make sure each fish is well coated.

4. Heat the vegetable oil to 170°C in a deep fryer or saucepan.

5. Add the whitebait and cook for 1-2 minutes until they start to turn golden.

6. Lift out with a slotted spoon and drain on kitchen paper.

7. Serve hot with lemon wedges, mayonnaise & chilli sauce.

Part 3 - Faceless fish and bottom feeders

GRAVAD LAX

Gravad lax is a Nordic (Nordic countries include Denmark, Norway, Sweden, Finland & Iceland) dish consisting of raw salmon, cured in salt, sugar, and dill. During the Middle Ages, gravad lax was made by fishermen, who salted salmon and cured it by burying it in the sand above the high-tide line.

Difficulty level 1

The name 'gravad lax' derives from the Scandinavian word grav, which literally means 'grave', and lax, which means 'salmon', so gravad lax literally means 'buried salmon'.

However, to make your own gravad lax a trip to the seaside is not necessary (nice but not a must). Instead we bury our fish in a marinade of salt, sugar and dill. The salmon cures by the act of osmosis. The moisture from the fish is drawn out and, with the salt/sugar mixture, creates a brine.

WHAT YOU'LL NEED… (SERVES 6)

- Large side of fresh salmon
- 2 large bunches of fresh dill
- 60g coarse salt
- 60g brown sugar
- 2 tablespoons crushed black peppercorns

HOW TO DO IT…

1. Place the salmon skin side down in a deep glass dish.

2. Spread dill over fish. Sprinkle dry ingredients over dill.

3. Cover with foil and press down with a board and a 5 pound weight (a small heavy object would be fine).

4. Refrigerate for 48 to 72 hours, turn the salmon and baste frequently.

5. Serve in very thin slices with rye bread, sour cream and lemon wedges.

PAELLA

Paella Spanish (pronounced pie ella) is a 19th century Valencian rice dish which originated near lake Albufera, in Valencia, on the east coast of Spain.

Difficulty level 2

Every Spanish cook/wife/mother has his or her own version of the perfect paella and good luck to anyone who dares to question a family recipe! Basically paella is white rice, vegetables and either meat or fish/seafood. Saffron (a spice derived from the crocus flower) is a key ingredient that distinguishes the dish as paella. Basically, you can add whatever you fancy to your paella. However, the recipe below is a really quick and simple prawn dish.

WHAT YOU'LL NEED… (SERVES 2)

- 350ml water
- 75g uncooked white rice
- 1 clove garlic, minced
- 450g fresh prawns, shelled and de-veined

- 300ml chicken stock
- 1 tin chopped tomatoes with juice
- 3 strands of saffron thread

HOW TO DO IT…

1. In a saucepan bring water to a boil. Add rice and stir.

2. Reduce heat, cover and simmer for 20 minutes.

3. Put a large frying pan over medium heat and then sauté (fry whilst constantly moving the pan around) the garlic and prawns for about 5 minutes or until the prawns are pink.

4. Pour in the stock, tomatoes and saffron; bring to a boil, stirring frequently. Stir in cooked rice and turn the heat right down. Cook for an additional 5 minutes.

5. Serve straight away. Salad is great with this dish.

Kipper Sandwiches

A kipper is a whole herring that has been gutted and then split from tail to head. It is salted or pickled, before being cold-smoked. Nowadays people tend to eat kipper for breakfast. However, before World War II they were popular treats for high tea.

Difficulty level 1

'Kipper time' is the season in which fishing for salmon in the River Thames is forbidden, by an Act of Parliament, in Great Britain, This is usually the period 3rd May to 6th January.

There are many stories of who created the first kippers and where, but we do know that kippers have been around for hundreds of years. By preserving the fish through salting and smoking, the fish have a long shelf life. We haven't always had freezers and fridges to keep our food fresh.

A 'red herring' is a very heavily smoked and cured kipper. A 'red herring' is an expression relating to a tactic to draw attention away from something of significance.

What you'll need... (Serves 3)

- ☑ **3 whole kippers**
- ☑ **6 slices thick wholemeal bread**
- ☑ **Knob of butter**
- ☑ **Dijon mustard**
- ☑ **Mayonnaise**
- ☑ **Rocket leaves**

How to do it...

1. Place a frying pan on the stove and heat. Add a knob of butter.

2. When the butter melts, add the kippers and cook for 2 minutes on each side, until warmed all the way through.

3. Butter all the slices of bread lightly. On 3 add a light spread of mustard.

4. On the second 3, spread a good dollop of mayonnaise.

5. Prepare your sandwiches thus:

6. Mustard bread on the bottom.

7. Then add the kipper and then some rocket, then the mayonnaise bread.

8. Squash well, cut into triangles, serve hot.

GOAN FISH CURRY

Almost the staple food of Goa (India's smallest state, found in South West India) along with rice, this fish curry is just delicious.

Difficulty level 3

Tuna tastes especially good in Goan Fish Curry but you can use any fish with firm flesh.

WHAT YOU'LL NEED... (SERVES 4)

- ✓ **1kg fish, cleaned and cut into smallish pieces**
- ✓ **1 ½ inch lump of tamarind**
- ✓ **½ a cup of hot water from a kettle**
- ✓ **1 large onion, sliced**
- ✓ **1 large tomato, sliced**
- ✓ **7 dried red chillies**
- ✓ **2 tablespoons of garlic paste or finely chopped garlic mushed with a fork or in a pestle and mortar**

- ✓ **1 tablespoon of ginger paste**
- ✓ **1 ½ cups of grated fresh coconut**
- ✓ **2 tablespoons of coriander powder, 2 tablespoons of cumin powder**
- ✓ **½ teaspoon of turmeric powder, ½ teaspoon of red chilli powder**
- ✓ **2 green chillies sliced in half**
- ✓ **2 tablespoons of vegetable oil**
- ✓ **Can coconut milk**

HOW TO DO IT...

1. Firstly, soak the tamarind in ½ a cup of hot water for 10 minutes.

2. Then, smash the tamarind with your fingers and mix it well into the water.

3. Strain through a sieve to extract all the pulp. Keep pulp aside.

4. Into a food processor or blender put the onion, tomato, coconut, ginger, garlic, dry red chillies, all the spices and the tamarind purée.

5. Blend to make a smooth paste. This is known as masala.

6. Heat a deep pan on a medium flame, add the oil.

If you like your curry hot, then add a couple of extra chillies - or take a couple out if you prefer a milder curry.

7. Add the green chillies and the masala paste and fry for 5 minutes.

8. Now add the can of coconut milk.

9. Bring to the boil then turn the heat down and reduce to a simmer. Cook for 15 minutes.

10. Season, with salt, to your taste.

11. Gently add the pieces of fish and cook for 10 minutes. Do not cover the pan at any time during the cooking.

12. Serve piping hot with plain boiled rice.

FISH BOURRIDE

La Bourride is one of the great classic fish dishes of Provence, France. It's a bit time-consuming to make – but not hard. It's definitely worth the effort.

Difficulty level 3

WHAT YOU'LL NEED… (SERVES 4)

- ✅ 1kg firm skinned & filleted white fish (cod, brill, turbot, monkfish etc)
- ✅ 2 leeks, sliced into thin rounds
- ✅ 1 finely sliced onion
- ✅ 500g of potatoes, peeled and sliced
- ✅ 2-3 cloves garlic, crushed
- ✅ 900ml fish stock

- ✅ 150ml dry white wine
- ✅ Freshly ground black pepper
- ✅ 4-6 slices French bread, toasted or fried in olive oil with garlic
- ✅ 1-2 tablespoons chopped parsley to garnish
- ✅ Garlic mayonnaise (otherwise known as aioli - see below)

FOR THE AIOLI…

- ✅ 6 cloves garlic
- ✅ 1 pinch of salt
- ✅ Freshly ground black pepper

- ✅ 2 egg yolks
- ✅ 300ml olive oil
- ✅ Squeeze of lemon juice

HOW TO MAKE AIOLI…

1. Place the garlic cloves on the chopping board. Sprinkle with salt and chop finely, then using your knife as a flat tool, press the garlic into a smooth paste.

2. Put into a mixing bowl.

3. Add the egg yolks and beat with a wooden spoon.

4. Add the oil drop by drop, beating all the time, and continue until the sauce thickens and all the oil is incorporated.

5. When the mixture is smooth and creamy, beat in some fresh lemon juice and ground black pepper to taste.

There's a reason some dishes stand the test of time. This is a classic.

HOW TO MAKE LA BOURRIDE...

1. Wash the fish fillets, pat them dry with kitchen paper and cut them into large pieces.

2. Put the leeks, onion and potatoes into a large shallow poaching pan with the garlic. Arrange the pieces of fish on top and pour in the fish stock and wine.

3. Poach gently, but do not boil, until the fish is just cooked.

4. Using a perforated spoon, remove the fish to a warmed serving dish and keep warm.

5. Bring the remaining stock up to boiling point and boil hard to reduce it to half of its original volume.

6. During this time, remove the potatoes when they are tender and keep warm with the fish.

7. Put 300ml of the aioli into a saucepan and warm over a very gentle heat.

8. Strain the reduced stock, then slowly pour it into the aioli, whisking all the time.

9. Gently bring the soup up to just under simmering point do not boil. It should be thick, pale and creamy.

10. Put a slice of toasted bread into individual large shallow soup bowls and arrange the pieces of fish and slices of potato on top.

11. Pour the soup all around the fish.

12. Serve straight away, with the rest of the aioli in a separate dish.

CRAB LINGUINI

You get two kinds of meat from Crabs. The brown meat which comes from the head has a stronger, fishier flavour and a sloppier texture. The white meat, mostly from the claws, is more delicate and firm.

WHAT YOU'LL NEED… (SERVES 4)

- ✅ 200g white crab meat
- ✅ 100g brown meat
- ✅ 2 cloves garlic
- ✅ 1 tablespoon of sea salt
- ✅ 1 large red chilli

- ✅ 125ml of extra virgin olive oil
- ✅ 1 lemon both juice and zest
- ✅ 500g linguine pasta
- ✅ 3 tablespoon of fresh chopped parsley

HOW TO DO IT…

1. Put a large pan of water on to boil for the pasta.

2. Place the garlic cloves on your chopping board, sprinkle with the salt. Chop finely then using the flat edge of your knife squish and grind to a smooth paste.

3. Add the chopped, seeded chilli and crush again.

4. Transfer to a bowl.

5. Tip the crab meat into the garlic/chilli mixture, breaking it up gently with a fork, and pour in the oil. Add the lemon zest, then the juice. Mix well.

6. Cook your pasta, drain and tip into a warmed serving bowl.

7. Immediately pour over the crab sauce and toss the pasta about in it, then throw in the parsley. Toss and serve.

8. Serve alone or with a fresh green salad.

Pasta, seafood and a bit of chilli heat – the perfect combo.

FISH

To save burned fingers you can use an empty shell as a 'mussel grabber' - and it's quite fun too!

MOULES MARINIERE
(MUSSELS IN WHITE WINE, CREAM & GARLIC)

Difficulty level 3

As with all shellfish, except shrimps, mussels should be checked to ensure they are still alive just before they are cooked.

There are enzymes that quickly break down the meat and make them unpalatable and sometimes dangerous after dying.

An easy trick to find out whether a mussel is alive is this: live mussels, when in the air, will shut tightly when disturbed. So tap one on the side and see if it clams together even more tightly than before. Ready-opened mussels should be discarded.

What you'll need... (Serves 4)

- 25g butter
- 2 shallots finely chopped
- 2 garlic cloves, finely chopped
- 1 bay leaf, freshly ground black pepper
- 2 stalks of fresh parsley
- 150ml dry white wine
- 1kg mussels in shell, scrubbed and beards removed
- 4 tablespoon crème fraîche

How to do it...

1. Melt the butter in a large heavy saucepan, add the onion and cook gently for 5 minutes until soft.

2. Add the garlic and parsley stalk then add the bay leaf and cook for a further minute.

3. Pour in the wine and bring to a fast boil.

4. Add all the mussels and cover the pan with a tight-fitting lid.

5. Cook over a medium heat, shaking the pan occasionally, for 3–5 minutes until the mussels have opened.

6. Take out and throw away the bay leaf and the parsley stalks.

Very important - after cooking you must throw out unopened mussels – they must not be eaten as this means they were dead when they went into the pan.

7. Strain the cooking juices through a fine sieve into a small saucepan.

8. Add the crème fraîche.

9. Add a handful of chopped fresh parsley.

10. Boil for a further 2 minutes. Then add black pepper to your taste.

11. Serve the mussels in warmed serving dishes and pour over the hot sauce.

12. Great with chips or big hunks of fresh white bread.

FISH

ROASTED SCALLOPS WITH EXOTIC SALSA

Difficulty level 3

The name scallops comes from the old French word escalope, which means 'shell'.

Scallops consist of two types of meat inside a brightly coloured fan shaped shell. The adductor muscle, called 'scallop', which is white and meaty, and the roe, called 'coral', which is red or white and soft.

Scallops have between 50 and 200 eyes around the front inside of its shell, almost like a string of beads. These eyes, however, respond only to light or dark, such as a shadow if a predator is approaching, prompting the scallops to snap shut.

WHAT YOU'LL NEED... (SERVES 4)

- ☑️ 75g pineapple, diced
- ☑️ 75g mango, diced
- ☑️ 50g cucumber, peeled and diced
- ☑️ 75g red pepper, diced
- ☑️ Tablespoons of chopped fresh coriander
- ☑️ 2 dessertspoons fresh lime juice
- ☑️ 1 green chilli, seeded and minced
- ☑️ Salt and freshly ground black pepper
- ☑️ 12 king scallops, coral removed, sliced in half horizontally

HOW TO MAKE AIOLI...

1. Mix the pineapple, mango, cucumber, red pepper, coriander, lime juice & chilli together in a bowl.

2. Season with salt and pepper then set aside.

3. Heat a large lightly oiled frying pan over medium-high heat.

4. On a flat plate drizzle some vegetable oil and season it with salt and pepper.

5. Place the scallops on the plate and coat with the seasoned oil.

6. When the pan is hot, sear the scallops until golden brown on both sides, about 2 minutes per side.

7. Plate the scallops. Spoon the salsa over the scallops, and serve immediately.

The scallops only need a couple of minutes either side, to get a lovely golden brown colour to them.

Pan fried Red Mullet, Basil & Olives

Not only an unfortunate hairstyle much-loved by 1980s footballers like Glenn Hoddle and Chris Waddle, the mullet is actually a species of goatfish. The red mullet is not related to the grey mullet. The red mullet can be found in the Mediterranean Sea, the North Atlantic Ocean and the Black Sea. When buying, ask your fishmonger to remove the pin bones.

What you'll need... (Serves 4)

- ✓ 3 tablespoons of vegetable oil
- ✓ 12 peeled shallots cut in halves
- ✓ 1 tablespoons of granulated sugar
- ✓ 2 tablespoons of balsamic vinegar
- ✓ 1 small garlic clove, crushed
- ✓ 50g pitted black olives, halved

- ✓ 30g pine nuts, toasted (with a little sprinkle of icing sugar is great)
- ✓ 1 tablespoon of olive oil
- ✓ 8 red mullet fillets, skin on, pin bones removed
- ✓ Small handful fresh basil leaves

How to do it...

1. Sprinkle your packet of pine nuts into a baking tray – **no oil**. Sprinkle a couple of pinches of icing sugar over the top and place on the top shelf of a hot oven. Roast until golden brown. Keep an eye on them. One second they look uncooked the next they are burned to a crisp!

2. Heat 1 tablespoon of vegetable oil in a medium saucepan. Add the shallots and brown all over. Add the sugar, balsamic vinegar and garlic and continue to cook for 10 minutes or until the shallots are soft. Then remove from the heat.

3. Stir through the olives, toasted pine nuts, olive oil and season with ground black pepper. Remove from heat and place in clean, dry bowl.

4. Heat a large, non-stick frying pan. On a flat plate, season some vegetable oil.

5. Place the red mullet on the plate and turn over, ensuring that the fillets are covered. Put the fillets, skin-side down, in the pan and cook for 3-4 minutes, until the skin is crispy.

6. Turn them over and cook for a further 1 minute, then remove from the pan and repeat with the remaining 4 fillets. Mix the basil leaves into the shallot salad, divide between serving plates and top with the fish fillets.

Prawn Cocktail

Difficulty level 2

Symbolic of the 1970's, along with flares, sideburns and dodgy hair styles, the classic prawn cocktail usually consists of shelled prawns, Marie Rose sauce, and iceberg lettuce. It is usually served in a glass and more often than not with a light sprinkling of paprika.

Marie Rose is a favourite British sauce made from a blend of ketchup and mayonnaise.

The Mary Rose Ship is based in Portsmouth Historic Dockyard. Built between 1509 and 1511, she was a firm favourite of King Henry VIII.

After a long and successful career, she sank accidentally during an engagement with a French fleet in 1545. Her rediscovery and raising were important events in the history of nautical archaeology. The hull of the Mary Rose, after years of deciding how to bring her back to shore, was towed into Portsmouth Harbour in the evening of October 11th 1982.

What you'll need... (Serves 8)

- 3 tablespoons of tomato ketchup
- 9 tablespoons of mayonnaise
- Lemon juice from half a lemon
- A few drops of Tabasco sauce
- 800g cooked and shelled prawns
- 1 small cucumber
- 1 green apple
- 1 iceberg lettuce, shredded finely
- Salt and freshly ground pepper, ground paprika

FISH

How to do it...

1. Put on the Bee Gees – or any 1970's poptastic classic! Dance around the kitchen and sing into a hairbrush. Right, now you're ready to start cooking.

2. First make the Marie Rose sauce by beating together the ketchup, mayonnaise, lemon juice and Tabasco.

3. Dice the cucumber and apple and mix with the shredded lettuce. Place in the bottom of either 8 serving glasses or 1 large serving bowl.

4. Mix the prawns and Marie Rose sauce together and put a good healthy dollop of it on top of the lettuce mixture. Season with a nice big pinch of ground paprika.

(Sea) Bass in Tin foil

In France this method of cooking is called 'en papillotte'. Fish, vegetables and fruit can all benefit from this mixed up method of steaming and infusing.

Difficulty level 2

The name bass comes from the middle English word 'bars', meaning perch.

To put the word sea in front of bass to create sea bass is actually not necessary, which is why we were clever and put it in brackets, above. There is no other kind of bass. There's no freshwater bass and no river bass. Regular marketing in restaurants has created the 'sea' part and it's stuck.

What you'll need… (Serves 2)

- ☑ 1 whole sea bass (ask the fishmonger to clean and gut it but NOT fillet it)
- ☑ Salted butter
- ☑ Thyme sprigs and bay leaves
- ☑ ½ fresh lemon
- ☑ Salt and pepper
- ☑ 1 chopped shallot

How to do it…

1. Preheat your oven to 200°C.

2. Take a sheet of tin foil, slightly longer than your fish, and smear with butter.

3. Season the buttered tin foil with black pepper, salt, the herbs and shallot.

4. Lay the bass on top and place some more butter and herbs on top of the fish

5. Cover with another piece of foil of the same size and scrunch the ends together and upwards.

6. Lay the foiled fish on a baking tray and place in the hot oven for approximately 20 minutes

7. After 20 minutes, remove the fish very carefully. Open one end of the parcel, being careful of the steam, and slip a knife into the thickest part of the fish. As with most fish cookery, if the flesh is still translucent and sticking to the bone then it will need more cooking. Simply reseal the foil parcel and return to the oven until the meat is a solid white and a little flaky.

8. Serve simply with buttered new potatoes and salad.

The smell that hits you
when you open up the
parcel is incredible.

Absolutely delicious.

FISH

Who needs a bowl?!

CREAMY SALMON IN SPUDS

Difficulty level 3

WHAT YOU'LL NEED... (SERVES 4)

- 4 large baking potatoes
- Knob of butter
- 600g salmon diced into 1 inch cubes
- 2 handfuls peeled prawns
- 1 onion
- 1 carrot
- 1 stick celery

- Chopped chervil and parsley
- 750ml whole milk
- Crushed black pepper
- 2 cups grated cheddar cheese
- 75g flour
- 75g salted butter
- Salt and pepper

How to do it...

1. Firstly place all of the potatoes into a cold oven. Turn the oven on to 200°C and cook for approximately 1 ½ hours. When cooked remove from oven. This stage can be done well in advance, even a day. Just stick the cold potatoes in the fridge to keep fresh.

2. Place the salmon into a saucepan and cover with the milk. Roughly chop the vegetables and onions and add to the pan.

3. Put the pan on the stove and turn up the heat until it begins to simmer. Then remove from the heat.

4. After 5 minutes, drain the fish and vegetables away from the milk. The vegetables can be discarded, but not the milk…or the fish.

5. In a clean sauce pan, melt the 75g butter over a low heat. Add the 75g flour and stir well to make a thick paste.

6. Take off the heat and add a little of your fishy milk. Stir it in. Now add a little more and a little more – stirring it in all the time. Eventually you will reach a point where the paste has completely gone and there are no lumps.

7. Then add the rest of your milk and return to the heat. Slowly bring the mixture up to simmering point, stirring all the time. If, after about 20 minutes of simmering and stirring, it is not a nice creamy texture try adding a little sprinkle of flour at a time until it is. If it is too thick then add some more milk - normal milk is fine. If it is lumpy do not despair: either push the sauce through a sieve or gently whisk, without adding too much air, until all lumps have gone.

8. Season what is now a béchamel sauce with salt and pepper and throw in the prawns and most of the cheese, saving about a tablespoon for the finished dish., Allow to cook very gently for a further five minutes.

9. Remove from the heat and add the chopped chervil and parsley then add the diced, cooked salmon.

10. Cut the baked potatoes in half and scoop the potato flesh into a mixing bowl. Do not pierce the skin of the spud. Keep the empty skins to one side.

11. Add a good knob of butter to the potato in the bowl, add seasoning and then mash.

12. Spoon some of the salmon mixture into the skins until about 2/3rds full. Top off with a little of the mashed potato mixture. Sprinkle over a little of the remaining cheese.

13. Return to the oven for about a further 15 minutes until the potato on top starts to brown.

14. Eat the whole thing!

Interior of Marcus at The Berkeley

Recipes from Marcus Wareing

Marcus's interest in food stemmed from his father's family fruit and vegetable business that supplied schools and catering facilities in the North West of England, from the age of ten he used to help with the packing and would join his father on local deliveries.

In 1986 Marcus started a City and Guilds qualification at Southport Technical College before commencing his professional career at The Savoy, at the young age of 18.

Marcus has worked with many of the world's finest and celebrated chefs including Anton Edelman, Albert Roux, Pierre Koffmann and Gordon Ramsay in some of the world's finest restaurants including The Savoy, Le Gavroche, The Grand in Amsterdam, The Point in New York, Aubergine, Guy Savoy in Paris, L'Oranger, The Savoy Grill & Banquette and Pétrus.

After working as Chef Patron of Pétrus for 9 years, and earning it two Michelin stars, in 2008 Marcus took on the restaurant lease at the Berkeley hotel and re-launched the restaurant as Marcus Wareing at The Berkeley. In March 2014 Marcus Wareing at The Berkeley was re-launched as Marcus after an extensive renovation, which transformed the once familiar claret dining room into a stunning new contemporary space.

In May 2011 Marcus Wareing launched his second restaurant, The Gilbert Scott at London's St Pancras Renaissance Hotel. September 2014 will see Marcus Wareing open his third restaurant, Tredwell's, the restaurant will be a vibrant West End Eatery located on Upper St Martin's Lane in the buzzing Seven Dials.

Marcus is a well know face on UK television and has appeared on a number of cookery shows including The Great British Menu, where he cooked the dessert for the Queen's 80th birthday and later went on to join the show as a veteran. More recently he has appeared on the BBC's Master Chef as a guest judge and in June 2014 it was announced that Marcus would be the new head judge on Master Chef: The Professionals.

Marcus lives in South London with his wife and three children.

A FEW WORDS FROM
MARCUS WAREING
CHEF / PATRON OF MARCUS AT THE BERKELEY, KNIGHTSBRIDGE.

Fish is probably one of my favourite ingredients. Since I first became a chef I must have filleted thousands of them with at least a hundred a day at The Savoy as a young chef. Preparing and cooking a piece of fish is possibly one of my favourite tasks in the kitchen purely because I have such respect for this amazing ingredient.

Nowadays we can easily buy many varieties of fish on a daily basis in our supermarkets but I think it is imperative that we consider the source, sustainability and seasonality of the fish. Not only to ensure that we can continue to enjoy them but more importantly so that the species can survive.

Faceless Fish and Bottom Feeders is a fantastic and informative journey for keen cooks of any age. It will inspire, intrigue and also encourage readers to sample the delights of the sea whilst giving due respect to this precious product.

Knowledge is key and this book provides it in a fun and interesting way, perfect for both children and adults alike. I shall certainly ensure my three children have a copy as they continue to learn to cook with enjoyment, understanding and respect.

Marcus Wareing

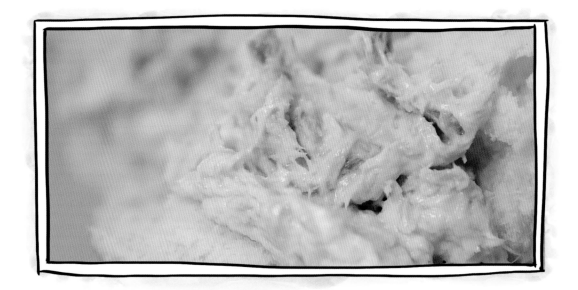

Smoked mackerel pâté

Difficulty level 1

This is a very tasty and easy recipe. It keeps well for a few days in the fridge too so is useful for lunches, or for snacking! Mackerel are also such a beautiful fish with their patterned blue and silver skin.

What you'll need... (Serves 4)

- ✔ **250g smoked mackerel fillet, skin and bones removed, flaked**
- ✔ **25g crème fraîche**
- ✔ **50g cream cheese**
- ✔ **25g good-quality mayonnaise**

- ✔ **Grated zest and juice of ½ lemon**
- ✔ **½ teaspoon salt**
- ✔ **Freshly ground black pepper**

How to do it...

1. Mix together the crème fraîche, cheese and mayonnaise until smooth.

2. Add the lemon zest and juice, salt and a few good turns of pepper. Add the mackerel and fold through the mix. Check the seasoning and adjust if necessary.

3. Serve on a sandwich, with chargrilled toast or your favourite crusty bread.

ROASTED MONKFISH WITH CHERRY TOMATO LENTILS

Difficulty level 3

WHAT YOU'LL NEED FOR THE MONKFISH… (SERVES 4)

- 24 portions monkfish tail (weighing approximately 150g each)
- 2 tablespoons vegetable oil
- 50g unsalted butter
- ½ teaspoon table salt

WHAT YOU'LL NEED FOR THE ACCOMPANIMENT…

- 300g cooked green lentils
- 1 onion, peeled and sliced
- 3 tablespoons vegetable oil
- 1 clove garlic, crushed
- 2 tablespoons tomato purée
- 1 tablespoon balsamic vinegar
- 1 tablespoon honey
- 300g ripe cherry tomatoes, halved
- ¼ bunch flat leaf parsley, chopped
- ½ teaspoon table salt
- ½ teaspoon coarsely ground black pepper

HOW TO DO IT…

1. For the beans, heat one tablespoon of vegetable oil until hot in a medium sized frying pan. Add the onions and garlic and cook until soft. Remove from the pan and set aside.

2. Add the other 2 tablespoons of vegetable oil and when smoking hot, add the cherry tomatoes and brown. Add the balsamic vinegar and cook for 2 minutes.

3. Add the onions back to the pan along with the tomato purée, salt and honey. Simmer gently then add the lentils and heat through. Add the chopped parsley just before serving.

4. To cook the monkfish; heat one tablespoon of vegetable oil in a frying pan over a moderate heat. Dust the monkfish with the salt then brown lightly all over.

5. Add the butter and continue cooking for around 5 minutes, until the fish is cooked. Serve immediately with the beans.

Yorkshire fishcakes with dill mayonnaise

Difficulty level 3

These fishcakes are really tasty. They are quite handy as you can make them a few hours before you need them, or even the day before, then store in the fridge until you need to cook them.

What you'll need for the fishcakes... (makes 6 fishcakes)

- ☑ 250ml milk
- ☑ ½ onion, peeled and finely chopped
- ☑ 1 bay leaf
- ☑ 200g natural smoked haddock fillet, skin off
- ☑ 20g unsalted butter
- ☑ 25g plain flour, plus extra for coating
- ☑ 1 tablespoon chopped chives

- ☑ 1 tablespoon chopped parsley leaves
- ☑ Grated zest and juice of ¼ lemon
- ☑ 1 hard-boiled egg, grated
- ☑ 200g potato, peeled, cubed and cooked through
- ☑ 1 tablespoon capers, chopped
- ☑ 1 egg, well beaten
- ☑ 100g panko breadcrumbs
- ☑ Oil for frying

& FOR THE MAYONNAISE...

- ✓ **2 egg yolks**
- ✓ **½ teaspoon Dijon mustard**
- ✓ **½ teaspoon English mustard (jar, not powder)**
- ✓ **2 tablespoons white wine vinegar**
- ✓ **50ml olive oil**
- ✓ **150ml vegetable oil**
- ✓ **2 tablespoons finely chopped dill**
- ✓ **Salt and white pepper**

HOW TO DO IT...

1. Put the milk, onion and bay leaf in a saucepan. Add the haddock and bring to a simmer, then poach the haddock until just cooked.

2. Remove the fish and set aside; strain and reserve the milk.

3. Melt the butter in a saucepan and stir in the flour to form a roux. Add the poaching milk, a ladle at a time, whisking continuously, until you have a thick white sauce (you may not need all of the milk). Cook over a gentle heat until the floury taste disappears, then set aside.

4. Flake the fish and potatoes into large chunks. Add to the sauce along with the herbs, lemon zest and juice, hard-boiled egg and capers.

5. Mix gently together, cover and place in the fridge to cool. When cool, roll into 6 balls and flatten with your hand. Cover and place back into the fridge.

6. To make the mayonnaise, whisk together the egg yolks, mustards and vinegar in a bowl until well combined, then slowly trickle in the mixed oils, whisking all the time, until a thick consistency is reached. Season to taste and mix through the dill.

7. Heat the oven to 180°C. Dip each cake in flour, then into beaten egg and finally into the breadcrumbs to coat evenly.

8. Shallow fry the fishcakes over a medium heat for 2-3 minutes each side then place in the oven to heat through. Serve hot with dollops of mayonnaise around.

FISH

Gower Peninsula Fisherman's stew

Difficulty level 3

These fishcakes are really tasty. They are quite handy as you can make them a few hours before you need them, or even the day before, then store in the fridge until you need to cook them.

What you'll need... (Serves 4)

- [✓] 1 bulb fennel, halved
- [✓] 2 large potatoes, peeled and cut into 3cm cubes
- [✓] 200g skinless pollock fillet, cut into bite-sized pieces
- [✓] 100g salmon or sea trout fillet, cut into bite-sized pieces
- [✓] 100g fish bones

& for the broth...

- [✓] 2 tablespoons vegetable oil
- [✓] 1 onion, peeled and halved
- [✓] 2 carrots, peeled and halved across
- [✓] 1 bulb garlic, halved horizontally
- [✓] 3 sticks celery, halved across
- [✓] 4 tablespoons tomato purée
- [✓] Pinch of saffron threads
- [✓] 1 leek, white part only, halved across
- [✓] ¼ bunch of tarragon
- [✓] ¼ bunch of thyme
- [✓] 2 litres chicken stock
- [✓] ½ teaspoon salt

How to do it...

1. Heat the vegetable oil in a large saucepan. When hot, add the fish bones, onion, carrots, garlic, leek and celery. Brown well, stirring constantly. Add the tomato purée and saffron, then the herbs and stock, bring to the boil. Simmer gently for 20 minutes.

2. Pass through a fine sieve into a clean pan, discarding the vegetables and fish bones. Bring to a gentle simmer, add the salt, potatoes and fennel and cook until almost tender.

3. Add the fish and simmer gently until just cooked – approximately 4-6 minutes. Serve with your favourite crusty bread.

FISH

Cod, leek and cheddar cheese pies

Difficulty level 3

What you'll need... (makes 4 individual pies)

- 500g sustainably fished cod (Atlantic or Pacific for example)
- 2 leeks, white part only, sliced
- 50g unsalted butter
- 100ml chicken stock
- 125g Cheddar cheese, grated
- 400ml semi skimmed or whole milk
- 100ml fish or chicken stock
- ¼ bunch thyme

- ½ bulb garlic, halved crossways
- 1 bay leaf
- ½ bunch flat leaf parsley, chopped
- 50g unsalted butter
- 50g plain flour
- ¼ teaspoon table salt
- 1 medium free range egg yolk
- 4 puff pastry discs, 3mm thick, to cover 1cm over the rim of your pie dishes

How to do it...

1. Place the milk, first measure of stock, thyme, garlic and bay leaf in a deep frying pan and warm gently, do not boil.

2. Season the cod then add to the liquid and allow to gently poach for around 5-8 minutes until it is just cooked through and flakes easily. Remove and set on paper towels. Strain the poaching liquor through a fine sieve and reserve.

3. Place the first measure of butter in a deep frying pan over a moderate-to-high heat. Add the leeks, season well and cook for 3-4 minutes until lightly coloured. Add the chicken stock and cook the leeks for a remaining 5 minutes until almost cooked through, set aside.

4. Melt the second measure of butter in a medium sized saucepan over a moderate heat. Whisk in the flour and cook for a couple of minutes. Add a little of the poaching liquor and whisk well. Add the remaining liquor and continue to cook gently until it has thickened and lost the raw flour taste.

5. Divide the cod, leeks and cheese evenly between the 4 pie dishes. Add the parsley to the white sauce, adjust seasoning if necessary then spoon into the pie dishes. Brush the top of the inside of the dishes with the egg yolk then lay the pastry over the top, sealing it at the top edge and over the dish. Slice the excess pastry off. At this stage either place the pies in the fridge to bake later or preheat the oven to 180°C.

6. Before baking, brush the pastry with egg yolk and make two slits for the steam to escape. Bake for 20-25 minutes until pastry is golden. Allow to rest for a couple of minutes before serving.

WARMING UP

In cooking terms, a conventional oven is a piece of kitchen equipment which is used for baking, heating, casseroling or roasting all kinds of food.

The typical kinds of oven, found it kitchens today, run on either gas or electricity. Some Rayburn or Aga style models can also run on oil and supply the house with hot water. It is also possible to get camping ovens that run on bottled gas.

A fan oven uses a fan to generate heat, rather than an electrical element. It warms up to the temperature that you have selected, then the fan distributes the hot air into the oven. They can be noisier than non-fan ovens, but reach the desired temperature quicker and spread the warm air evenly. An oven that uses just elements will heat from the bottom or, as a grill, from the top.

Before you cook something, unless otherwise mentioned, your oven needs to be heated to the required temperature. It may only take a minute to turn it on, but it will take a while for it to reach the right temperature. Often your oven will have a red or green light that will go off when it has reached the temperature you have set.

Modern ovens usually have a large compartment at the bottom and a smaller one at the top. These are usually controlled independently of each other. The top oven normally acts as a grill, as well as a small oven chamber.

A microwave oven is an oven which uses micro radiation waves as a heat source, instead of a fire source. Microwaves were first invented in 1946 and are most commonly used today to defrost things quickly, or to warm things up quickly. Though they can be used as a whole cooking method, most people prefer to use regular ovens.

The oldest ovens found to date were from Central Europe and dated back to 29,000 BC. They were found to be inside yurts and were roasting pits used to cook mammoth.

GLOSSARY

Saucepan

A metal, heat-treated glass or enamel pan with a long handle. Most households will have a pan set of 3 differing sizes. Pans usually have lids, which assist in bringing things up to temperature quickly.

Frying Pan

A shallow, flat-bottomed and long-handled pan, used for frying food.

Wok

A large metal pan with a rounded bottom, mostly used in Asian cooking for frying and steaming.

Baking Sheet

Mostly made of aluminium or stainless steel, these are flat rectangular pans that are used in the oven for baking.

Roasting Pan

A roasting pan is designed to withstand the very high heat encountered in an oven. Roasting pans can be made from enamel, ceramic, metal, or heat-treated glass.

Casserole dish

The word casserole comes from the French word for 'saucepan'. It is a large, deep dish used both in the oven and also as a vessel in which to serve food. The word 'casserole' can also be used for the food cooked and served in such a dish.

Pie dish

Shallower than a casserole dish, this is usually made of heat-treated glass or ceramic and has side lips that slant away.

Mandolin

This is a piece of slicing equipment that has a flat frame and adjustable blades. It is incredibly sharp and users should exercise caution. As with a grater, you should endeavour to keep your hands flat when using and slice away from your body.

Sieve

This consists of a wire or plastic mesh suspended in a frame. It is used for straining solids from liquids or for separating larger and smaller particles. It can also be used to reduce soft solids to a pulp when making purées or smooth mash.

Colander

Larger than a sieve, a colander is usually made from metal or plastic and is used to strain hot liquid away from cooked foods such as vegetables and pasta.

Pastry brush

A wooden, or plastic-handled brush used for painting egg, oil or milk wash. Make sure the brush does not lose its 'hairs' easily.

Kitchen Roll

We all know what kitchen roll is, and the only thing we have to mention is this: please do not be tempted to use toilet roll in place of kitchen roll as it can stick to food. Rather, use a clean dry tea towel.

Teaspoonful

A teaspoonful equates to 5ml.

Tablespoonful

A tablespoonful equates to 15ml.

Dessertspoonful

A dessertspoonful equates to 10ml.

Pinch

Used for dry ingredients and common with seasoning as it can be more, or less, than a simple pinch, according to taste. Using your thumb and index finger, 'pinch' some of the ingredients you are adding and sprinkle into or onto the dish you are creating.

Knob

Usually refers to a walnut-sized lump of butter.

Slice

Cutting longways, for example down the length of a carrot.

Chop

Cutting across the thinnest part of your ingredient, for example across a carrot.

Peel

To remove, using a small knife, the outer skin, stalk and root of a vegetable. Alternatively, to remove casings from shellfish.

Boil

When referring to a liquid, this mean it reaches the temperature at which it makes large bubbles.

Simmer

This stays just below the boiling point and has very tiny bubbles, unlike the large boiling ones.

Caramelise

This happens when carbohydrates like sugar or meat are heated to extremely high temperatures, which causes them to turn brown and can add rich flavours.

Browning

This is when you cook only the surfaces of the meat. Usually done on a high heat, it gives the meat an attractive colour, removes excess fat and develops a deep flavour.

Poaching

The word poach means to cook something in a liquid. Usually it is reserved for delicate items like eggs and fish. However other meats such as chicken and vegetables can also be poached.

Steaming

A method of cooking using steam which works by boiling water in a pan with a lid on, thus creating steam. The steam carries heat to the food to cook it. There is no contact with the food and the water, only the steam.

Deglaze

This means to add liquid such as stock or wine to a pan (typically after roasting meat or fish in it) to loosen the heavily-flavoured, caramelised pieces stuck to the bottom.

Acknowledgments

Creating this book would have been extremely difficult without the help, support and love from a number of people. The creation of the first volume of Gastronomical! has been an exciting adventure and, at times, we have both annoyed the pants off and chewed the ears off many friends and family.

There are many people to thank but, notably, there are a few we must mention. Gemma Reece, who patiently assisted in the arduous task of recipe testing and photographing the food. Simon, Kevin, the Rowleys and the Holloways, who were called in to guinea pig the completed dishes. Sarah Astbury, who held our hands all the way through and Lucy Bennell & Josh Tuifua who were there at the start of this concept and who metaphorically kicked our butts to push on with it. And of course the children, Paige, Scarlett, Isabelle, Alfie and George who enjoyed a food fight in the garden at the end of the photo shoot.

We must also thank Chefs Tom Kerridge, Marcus Wareing, Shaun Hill and Claude Bosi for their contributions. It's easy to forget, when you see them on hot headed cookery shows, that they too were children once. All of the Chefs have supported this book and its message. The one common factor that links them all is the fact they all enjoyed and appreciated food from an early age. One thing they all mentioned throughout the process of writing this, is the worry that food is rarely taught at school and parents don't necessarily have the time to do so at home. We must also thank Paul Goodfellow for his fantastic plate ware used during the photo shoot.

We are deeply indebted to Dave Webb and Rob March of We are Beard for the incredible illustrations and design of the book. The work both Dave and Rob have done has brought the book to life and their joy and enthusiasm in creating this with us is apparent throughout. They are without doubt, two of the most visionary people on this planet.

Last, but far from least, we are beholden to our patient and painstaking editor / photographer / publisher, Andrew Richardson of A Way With Media. Andrew's considerable contributions, both professionally and personally, his belief in the message we are hoping to get across to families and his unflappable ability to work to any deadline, made the publication of this book possible. He also has a good taste in music.

Thank you all xx